the architect's office

the architect's office

Anatxu Zabalbeascoa

Whitney Library of Design
An imprint of Watson-Guptill Publications
New York

To Miguel, for so many workshops shared.

Acknowledgments
I would like to thank the following individuals and institutions for their help in preparing this book:
Mónica Gili, for advice, assistance, support, and ecouragement; Eulalia Coma, for her design; Miguel Ruano, for documentation and discussions of office buildings; Javier Rodrìguez-Marcos, for his suggestions and the final reading of the text; Carmen Hernández Bordas and Jon Hicks, for carrying out some assignments; Jorge Lozano, director of the Academy of Spain in Rome, for his support while I wrote the text; and the libraries of the College of Architects of Barcelona and the American Academy in Rome for the use of their collections. Last, I am grateful to the architects who met with me during the writing of this book, to those who appear in it as well as those who, in the end, I could not include.

© 1996 Editorial Gustavo Gili S.A., Barcelona

First published in the United States by Whitney Library of Design, an imprint of Watson-Guptill Publications, a division of BPI Communications, Inc., 1515 Broadway, New York, NY, 10036.

English translation by Ernst van Haagen, Bertrand Languages Inc.

Library of Congress Cataloging-in-Publication Data

Zabalbeascoa, Anatxu.
  [Taller del arquitecto. English]
  The architect's office / by Anatxu Zabalbeascoa.
    p.   cm.
  Includes index.
  ISBN 0-8230-0233-0
  1. Architectural offices—Planning. 2. Architectural offices—Decoration. 3. Office layout. I. Title.
  NK2195.04Z2313 1996
  725'.33—dc20   96-22313
                                                  CIP

Manufactured in Spain

First printing, 1996

1 2 3 4 5 6 7 8 9 / 02 01 00 99 98 97 96

Contents

Introduction — 6

Tadao Ando, Kita, Osaka, 1991 — 18

Baufrösche, Kassel, 1993 — 22

Ricardo Bofill, Sant Just Desvern, Barcelona, 1973–1975 — 28

Mario Botta, Lugano, Ticino, 1990 — 34

Coop Himmelblau, Vienna, 1975 — 40

Alexandre Chemetoff, Gentilly, Paris, 1995 — 42

David Chipperfield, London, 1989 — 48

Terry Farrell, London, 1987 — 54

Norman Foster, London, 1990 — 56

Frank O. Gehry, Santa Monica, California, 1988 — 62

Michael Graves, Princeton, New Jersey, 1982 — 68

Vittorio Gregotti, Milan, 1972 — 70

Nicholas Grimshaw, London, 1993 — 74

Gwathmey Siegel, New York, 1982 — 78

Zaha Hadid, London, 1985 — 80

Agustín Hernández, México, D.F., 1972–1975 — 84

Michael Hopkins, London, 1994 — 88

Arata Isozaki, Tokyo, 1985 — 94

Josef Paul Kleihues, Berlin, 1986 — 98

Ricardo Legorreta, México, D.F., 1966 — 102

Yves Lion, Paris, 1990 — 106

Mecanoo, Delft, 1995 — 110

Richard Meier, New York, 1986 — 112

Enric Miralles and Benedetta Tagliabue, Barcelona, 1990 — 116

Morphosis, Santa Monica, California, 1993 — 122

Jean Nouvel, Paris, 1995 — 126

Dominique Perrault, Paris, 1990 — 130

Renzo Piano, Vesima, Genoa, 1994 — 134

Richard Rogers, London, 1984–1989 — 140

Harry Seidler, Sydney, 1973–1989 — 144

SITE, New York, 1984 — 150

Alvaro Siza, Oporto, 1996 — 154

Robert A.M. Stern, New York, 1985 — 156

Oscar Tusquets, Barcelona, 1992 — 158

Oswald Mathias Ungers, Cologne, 1958–1989 — 164

Venturi, Scott-Brown and Associates, Manayunk, Pennsylvania, 1980 — 168

Jean-Michel Wilmotte, Paris, 1991 — 172

Shoei Yoh, Tokyo, 1971 — 176

Biographies — 182

Photography Credits — 192

Paul Klee, *The Chosen Place,* 1927

M.C. Escher, *Hand with Reflective Sphere,* 1935

Giorgio Vasari, *Filippo Brunelleschi Presenting the Model of San Lorenzo to Cosimo the Elder,* 1563

Jacopo da Empoli, *Michelangelo Presenting the Façade of San Lorenzo to Pope Leon X and to Cardinal de Medici*

Introduction

The Advent of the Architect's Office

From ancient Greece to the Middle Ages, manual work was considered degrading, inferior to leisurely pursuits and a life of contemplation. While spaces like libraries were dedicated to intellectual work, manual labor was relegated to the closed and usually chaotic, disease-infested spaces of workshops. The laborers' resultant scars—callused hands, stooped shoulders, mental ailments caused by the oppressiveness of working conditions—came to characterize the appearance of the working class. Not until the work being done in these workshops was respected would the space itself claim any importance.

The first professions to lead the way were the goldsmiths, sculptors, and musicians, whose *ateliers* came to represent the very creativity of those who inhabited them. The goldsmiths, whose handcrafted jewelry was akin to art, particularly helped shape the space of the first architecture studios. Until the Middle Ages, architecture was the work of masons, carpenters, and stonecutters, who calculated the measurements of structures by a simple system based on the proportions of squares and triangles. The master builders were itinerant professionals who carried their gear on their backs. Bundled in with the few belongings of the builders, the early architectural "workshops" were unpacked on site, the workspace defined only by the tools grasped in the hands of their owners.

The Renaissance, however, brought a class of sophisticated architects, who turned to the classics in search of proportion, symmetry, and geometrical perfection. The creator of Renaissance churches and palaces was no longer a structural technician but instead an artist, on a par with painters and sculptors (many of whom were goldsmiths). Accustomed to calculating proportions and instructed in the pursuit of sculptural harmony, the early Renaissance architects were themselves workers in precious metals. Michelozzo was trained as a jeweler, later worked with Donatello, and ended his days as architect to Cosimo the Elder, of the Medici family.

Painters ventured into architecture as well, and their studios, with their high ceilings and ample daylight, were well suited to the work of designing buildings. Bramante was one of the most important architects who had been trained as a painter. Toward the end of his life, he envisaged a cupola for the Basilica of Saint Peter at the Vatican that would rival even the Pantheon in Rome. Upon his death in 1514, his pupil Raphael met the challenge. Following his work at the Villa Madarea and the Palazzo Pandolfini in Florence, Raphael designed a Papal basilica after Bramante at the Vatican. Though the project was never built, models of it (a rarity at

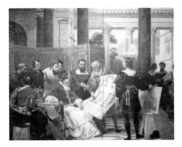

Horace Vernet, *Julio II and his Artists*

Bernardino Barbatelli, *La bottega del architetto*

Domenico Cresti, *Michelangelo Presenting the Model of San Pedro to the Pope*, 1619

Tommaso Manzuoli, *Two Men* 1556

the time) still exist. The painter Giulio Romano, a pupil of Raphael, became an architect when he moved to Mantua. There, among other projects, he built the Cathedral and the Ducal Palace. Giorgio Vasari, one of the painters who stubbornly resisted practicing architecture, eventually built an exhibition hall for paintings in Florence known as the Uffizi gallery, commissioned by the Duke of Tuscany.

The decline of practical experience in building construction as the sole indicator of architectural ability, along with a rise in the study of architectural theory, made possible a new vocation: the dilettante architect. One of the first was the humanist Leon Battista Alberti, who delegated many of his commissions to his more practically experienced assistants. Sebastiano Serlio abandoned painting entirely and devoted himself exclusively to the formulation of architectural theory. In the latter part of his life, Michelangelo, by training and vocation a sculptor, revolutionized architecture with his interpretation of the rules of design, renewing and simplifying all the elements of the architectonic idiom. After designing the Sacristy of the Church of San Lorenzo in Florence, he was awarded the commission of designing Saint Peter's for the Vatican. A painting done in 1619 by Domenico Cresti portrays the presentation of Michelangelo's model of Saint Peter's to Pope Paul IV. The archi-

tect, restored by the Renaissance to the higher creative rank, had finally attained the respect he deserved.

These same great models built during the Renaissance for entry in the many competitions of the time were the means of training numerous architects, who would subsequently graduate from the carpenter's workshop to the revamped architect's office. Antonio Manetti Ciaccheri began by constructing Brunelleschi's models, and ended up an expert in cupolas, inheriting commissions from his patron. The newly converted architect's office, more suited to the upward social turn in the profession, gradually incorporated libraries, which became as necessary a tool in the execution of good architecture as the compass and triangle. Pedro Machuca, another pupil of Raphael, brought this novelty to Spain, where he built one of the most remarkable works of the Spanish Renaissance, Charles V's palace in Granada.

In Italy, the Renaissance elevated the architect to professional status, while in the North, his knowledge was still intrinsically linked with engineering. Elsewhere in Europe, the evolution from craftsman to designer came about more slowly. In attaining the rank of artist, the architect had advanced from the early metalworking shop to occupy his own private workspace. As larger architectural firms were gradually founded, these offices became entre-

preneurial headquarters, with the added benefit of evoking status and prestige.

The Move to Modern Office Buildings
Toward the end of the eighteenth century, private offices were appended to the residences of merchants and professionals. Modeled after home libraries, these spaces felt open and inviting to clients, yet maintained enough privacy to permit concentration and discretion. Some offices went so far as to incorporate dining rooms and parlors, added luxuries for holding meetings and receiving clients.

Times were changing, however, and the fall of the Old Regime brought with it the social ascent of the bourgeoisie and the birth of modern capitalism. More important for the architect's office, though, were the advances in iron and steel building technologies developed during the Industrial Revolution. These allowed the emergence of a new structural genre, adapted to the new needs of intellectual laborers: the office building. The prestige of this technologically advanced building type catapulted the architect's office to the status of enterprise. The functional efficiency derived from this construction allowed other enterprises to share quarters in the same building, further bringing the architect's practice into the commercial mainstream.

Small private suites were first arranged along narrow corridors (as in the Old Colony building, Chicago, 1894, by archi-

Edward Hopper, *Nighttime Conversation,* 1949

Holabird & Roche, *Old Colony Building,* Chicago, 1894

tects Holabird & Roche). Liberated of heavy supporting walls by advances in structural steel and by new systems of artificial ventilation and lighting, the design of even the modest rental office building began to open and explore space in historically unprecedented ways. In the cities featuring these structures, we find examples of lightweight piles, which, as they grew ever lighter, shed the antiquated appearance of the first office buildings.

By the nineteenth century, a series of inventions, such as the Morse telegraph in 1844, the typewriter in 1868, and the telephone in 1876, signaled the progressive and irreversible introduction of technology into the workplace. The nineteenth century saw the birth of what we have come to regard as corporate architecture. Characteristic features of such structures became fixed: a hierarchical organization, equating rank with distance above ground; proximity to light; and height of ceilings.

The steel file cabinets and stainless steel tubular furniture of the 1920s changed the "look" of the modern office, most significantly through the standardization of parts and rearrangement and reorganization of usable space. Office furnishings themselves underwent the greatest change during the 1940s, when many architects, as partisans of functionalism, designed their own. Such firms as Knoll,

Herman Miller, and Thonet executed designs by Mies van der Rohe, Charles and Ray Eames, Eero Saarinen, Marcel Breuer, and others. Modular furniture systems and wall storage systems also became popular during those years.

Then, in 1946, the coming of the first computer, UNIAC, heralded a future of radical change in workplace architecture. To address the needs of office workers, a new profession emerged, one that fell somewhere between architecture and decorating and that would be responsible for the internal organization of the building. The practice of interior design would now determine the specification of such elements as carpeting and other accessories, the acoustic treatment of ceilings, and the placement of dividers between work areas.

One of the earliest examples of interior design in offices is the work of Frank Lloyd Wright for S.C. Johnson Wax in Racine, Wisconsin, in 1936. In this space Wright made the transition from conventional, compartmented and subdivided office to artfully crafted interior. The employees on the building's main floor enjoy very high ceilings, with no separation between work spaces. The perception of space is therefore enlarged. Another early example of interior design is the work of the Quickborner Group in Germany, designed in 1958. Claiming that the system of office

partitions stultifies office workers and limits productivity, Quickborner eliminated partitions—including those belonging to management personnel—and opened up spaces, recommended lighter-weight furniture for more flexible use in work areas, and suggested constant temperature and illumination levels.

This kind of humanization of the workplace was widely explored in architecture and interior design during the course of the 1970s. In this decade, "high tech" furnishings often took the place of antiques. Moldings and ornamental relief were eliminated in favor of Bauhaus-inspired industrial furniture made of steel tubing, which had been adopted in only a few buildings before that time. In addition, artificial lighting in the form of fluorescent tubes, along with artificial ventilation and air conditioning, added greatly to the maintenance costs of office buildings.

Adapting to the Contemporary Office

A number of occupations that were indispensable to the early-twentieth century office have been rendered practically obsolete by the computer: Filing clerks, librarians, stenographers, and even secretaries are less necessary because of new technology. The changes taking place in professional offices are happening so rapidly that one could compare it with the introduction of the assembly line and

Bristol United Press offices

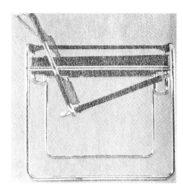

Marcel Breuer, *Wassily Chair,* 1923

automation in factories following the Industrial Revolution. While some have spoken out against the dehumanizing effects of technology in the modern workplace, it is clear that there is no going back. When files, accounting, drafting, appointments, and structural calculations can all be processed and stored in the same computer, there can be but few architects in the western world who have not yet computerized their offices.

The electronic and digital revolution has indeed left a visible mark on many buildings. In the past few years, architectural "high tech" has produced "smart" buildings which, with their futuristic look, are coming to be seen as the embodiment of a powerful new epoch, just as the neoclassical extravagances of nineteenth-century bank architecture were. Often companies that develop and use new technologies choose to have their buildings reflect those interests, such as in the case of Richard Meier's Canal Plus headquarters in Paris. The technology on display may be only a matter of form, since, paradoxically, it miniaturizes the computers and other hardware to the vanishing point. "Smart" buildings can be misleading; if anything is attributable to the electronic age in architecture, it is the decreased importance of the building itself.

Integration and flexibility are the new priorities in the architecture of contemporary offices. Designers now make an effort to create work spaces that will inspire managers and employees, in some cases by decentralizing work areas to encourage communication between workers. Some urban models have been used as references in visualizing the new typology. For instance, the Scandinavian Airlines offices in Stockholm encompass shops, restaurants, and other amenities commonly associated with leisure time. A similar strategy was employed by the Swedish designer Ralph Erskine in laying out The Ark, an office complex in London. This more inclusive planning strategy is intended to stimulate employees to higher productivity. Further experimentation with large volumes and unconventional building materials will continue to emphasize new priorities in the office, like communication, diversity, and diversion.

One of the few professions where hierarchy and prestige in the office are still ranked above interior comfort is banking. Bank offices—in trying to impart an image of strength and stability—have been the province of architectural postmodernism, which has sought to retrieve traditional architectural values of the past by imitating their forms. In addition to directly borrowing from the past, a well-known architect may be commissioned, in which case the project becomes an advertisement even before it is finished.

Offices Seeking an Image

Architecture has often helped provide businesses with a definitive and positive image. Sir John Soane transformed the closed pattern of bank architecture with his Bank of England (1790-1832) in London by specifying an unprecedented succession of skylighted rooms. The headquarters of the Hoechst chemical products company (1920), built by Peter Behrens in Frankfurt, functioned as such an effective image that Hoechst later incorporated it in its corporate logotype. Much as banks commissioned architects in the nineteenth century to design monumental, neoclassically styled structures that would echo the stability suggested by that idiom, in the twentieth century enterprises that pioneered technological advances have also used architecture to assert the modernity and inventiveness of their products. Frank Lloyd Wright's S.C. Johnson Wax headquarters (1936-1939) in Racine, Wisconsin, exemplifies the client's commitment to social and technological advancement. Wright's architecture—cleansed of traditional allusions, characteristically open, and encouraging a sense of community among the employees—symbolizes the company's entrepreneurial commitment to progress, good will, and sound business. Wright's creation put the Johnson Wax name on the pages of the magazines and newspapers of the time. Apart from

John Soane, *Bank of England*, 1788-1833

Frank Lloyd Wright, *Larkin Building*, Buffalo, 1904

Frank Lloyd Wright, *S.C. Johnson Wax Headquarters,* Racine, Wisconsin, 1936-1939

Reinhard, Hood & Fouilloux, Rockefeller Center, New York, 1932

the social features of the project—in the form of generous provision for overhead space, lighting, and traffic—structural details and the use of certain materials, such as the tubular Pyrex passage between two wings of the factory, are now regarded as architectural milestones, and have exerted a notable influence over later developments. Today, the history books pay tribute to the company's exemplary workplace, which is still in use.

During the 1950s, when the International Style was extending and expanding the influence of Modernism, the Lever House (1951) in New York, by the American firm of Skidmore, Owings & Merrill, and later the Seagram Building (1956), designed by Mies van der Rohe, sacrificed exterior expressiveness in favor of elements that facilitated function through the use of new construction techniques. Pragmatic criteria were shifting the impressiveness of a building from its façade to its size (and in the case of the United States, often to its height), subsequently changing the face of business and the visible features of architecture. The Sears Tower (1969-1974), erected by Skidmore, Owings & Merrill in Chicago, broke the height record for skyscrapers at 110 floors (1454 feet), overtopping the twin towers of the World Trade Center in New York (1967-1972) by Yamasaki and Roth, also 110 floors, but only 1350 feet high. Previous champions include the Empire State Build-

ing (1931) with 110 floors, 1250 feet; the Chrysler Building (1930) with 77 floors, 1046 feet; and, much earlier, far from Manhattan, the Eiffel Tower (1889), 1050 feet.

Moving away from the "bigger is better" school of thought, the new mode of individualizing structures emanated from the social concerns of the late seventies. Quality of work space became a fundamental element in a company's image. Economists, psychologists, and sociologists agreed that a good work environment would foster and increase worker productivity and morale. In that spirit, when Kevin Roche designed the Ford Foundation Building (1968) he created an enclosed garden, a little patch of greenery set among the highrises of Manhattan.

The seventies were to disseminate and popularize the social concerns addressed by Roche. Experiments in entrepreneurial techniques for stimulating worker motivation and participation were launched. Architecture, formerly preoccupied with offering a façade calculated to impress the public with an image of solvency and power, turned inward. Buildings now addressed interior spaces, the office workers' domain. Open office plans were the resultant design feature that characterized business administration. One of the most distinguished examples of this new spirit, the Centraal Bheer building (1972) in Apeldoorn, by the Dutch architect Herman

Hertzberger, opened the office to new ethical considerations by avoiding compartmentalization and transforming the office into a microworld with streets, stations, and places of business. Hertzberger's microcosm sought to abolish the sensation of living in a ghetto, a feeling experienced by office workers shut up in cold spaces that mandated solitary labor. His design benefited not only the occupants, and consequently the work they performed there, but also the image of the company that commissioned the architect. Projects like Centraal Beheer confirmed what had been learned from earlier administrative centers: A thoughtful and finished building is not more expensive than inferior alternatives, and in the long run, in terms of efficiency and company image, what benefits the employee is good for business.

Along similar lines of social responsibility, the Willis-Faber & Dumas building (1974) in Ipswich by Foster Associates represents a further step in bringing enterprise and employee together. This structure embodies the inapplicability of architectonic idioms related to any precedent. Stripped even of Modernism's visible structure, the façade reflects the sun during the day and reveals the inner activity at night. As a workplace, it continues the Centraal Beheer idea of a working community rather than isolated workers, with the

Mies van der Rohe and Philip Johnson, *Seagram Building*, 1958

E.K. Roche and J.G. Dinkerloo, *Ford Foundation Building*, 1965

Norman Foster, *Willis, Faber & Dumas Headquarters*, Ipswich, 1973-1974

Michael Graves, *Portland Building*, Portland, 1979-1982

expectation that comfort and convenience will directly improve business productivity. The emergence of new attitudes and new employee relations demanded a scenario for the development of such changes. By installing a swimming pool and creating employee recreation areas, Norman Foster pioneered a blending of leisure and labor.

The oil crisis marked a time of disillusionment, and coincided with the commencement of the electronic revolution. At the end of the seventies, still with the thought that architecture should address social concerns, Post Modernism undertook to restore the declarative importance of the façade, imitating elements of the past. In borrowing historical references, the new architecture once more adopted a hierarchically distributed interior. Historic edifices supplied the direct reference for Michael Graves when he left the New York Five group to erect an office building in Portland, Oregon, which gives priority to the prestigious image rather than to unity of design or well-being of the employees; the exterior windows—done in sheets of dark glass placed in front of concrete walls—do not match the actual size of the openings.

The prestigious headquarters building aspires to differentiate itself from the common run of rental structures. Professional workshops, studios, and offices comment on the work performed there, just as outward appearance lends clues to a person's personality. In the architect's own case, the office may serve not only to reflect the characteristics of his work, but also to provide a coherent sample of his creative range.

Offices Today

Much as Reyner Banham saw the post-industrial period in the *First Machine Age,* with means of production related to design, so the new means of communication and the diminishing size of electronic devices of ever greater capacity have given rise to a "second machine age." Virtual reality and data transmission may be generating yet a third stage in the machine age. This accelerated process of mechanization of labor requires the architect to develop fresh new spaces to accomodate changing professional needs.

As users of advanced present-day technology, most businesses combine the renovation and modernization of their facilities with the representation—the visual image—of all this updating. As a result, many prestigious offices have chosen the technological idiom for the architecture of their premises. The language of technology speaks of progress, information, timeliness, and security.

The angled skyscraper built by Norman Foster in Hong Kong for the Hong Kong & Shanghai Banking Corporation was reputed to be the world's most expensive building. Through the structure's extrinsic expression, Foster individualized the building, converting it into an icon while evoking the idea of the public plaza as a workplace. Richard Rogers, in building the Lloyds Bank headquarters in London, developed the features of the "smart" building to the maximum. The building not only is remarkably energy efficient, but is also distinguished from everything else in the City of London. Frank Gehry in turn imparted a new individuality to the office building, lending it the aspect of a work of art, sculptural object, or advertising display. Gehry used unusual materials in great volume to create extraordinary buildings like the American Center in Paris.

The current look in new construction is achieved in part by the use of materials pertaining to a particular period, or by the radical and innovative use of traditional materials. As was formerly the case with cathedrals, palaces, and town halls, architecture for work (offices and studios) and leisure (bars, hotels, restaurants, museums) today is based on new architectonic procedures. Platforms for experimentation tend to merge the seemingly opposed concepts of labor and leisure. These concepts seem destined to mingle for the better and more complete realization of both potentials: enjoyment of work, utilization of free time.

Norman Foster, *Hong Kong and Shangai Banking Corporation Headquarters,* Hong Kong, 1979-1984

Frank Gehry, offices and parking, Venice, California, 1989

Johannes Vermeer, *The Geographer,* 1669

Johannes Vermeer, *The Astronomer,* 1668

Architecture Offices

An architect's office is a business enterprise, and accordingly some in the profession choose spaces that express different aspects of their craft. Others work out of warehouse space, areas in which design activities pervade every corner and an intimacy with materials and tools reflects the architect's ambiguous position between artist and artisan.

Architects' offices, studios, workshops, showrooms, and places of business represent the entire spectrum of possible treatment of the work space. A number of architects use their offices as showplaces for architectural achievement or as galleries of creativity, and some elect to sacrifice privacy in the workplace in favor of openness. Others have preferred lofts, which they remodel and transform into storehouses of ideas. Recycling old industrial architecture (factories and warehouses) and typologically rearranging space (converting obsolete spaces into offices) lend the architect's work space a measure of ambiguity, making it difficult to classify it as studio, workshop, or office.

The thirty-eight examples included in this book offer an international survey of the architect's office. They represent a spectrum of schemes that range from fanciful structures to austere offices, domestic spaces, or workshops like those once used by cabinetmakers, carpenters, chan-

dlers, goldsmiths, printers, mechanics, and other manual craftspeople. Typically, workshops are chaotic spaces, unlike offices, which are usually more conducive to contemplation, reading, and study. The sample of spaces presented in this book illustrates the difficulty of classification. While frequently the architecture practiced and the place where it is created are at variance, many work spaces are difficult to classify just because they resist any particular label.

Perhaps the only architect's office included in this selection that does not fit the studio category is that of David Chipperfield in London. Carrying on the Victorian tradition of natural light in large work spaces and avoiding visual contact between the artist and the outdoors, Chipperfield encloses himself in the two great bays of his studio, escaping the distraction of any direct contact with the outside world. Control of the views seen from the studio is also a direct allusion to the Japanese architecture that has influenced Chipperfield's work so profoundly over the years.

The Baufrösche office in Germany continues the tradition of the *atelier.* A rural air and a formality of design suggest a workshop rather than a design office. Technology and artisanry interact to project the facial expression of a design "factory," characteristic of the Baufrösche, who have executed noteworthy restructur-

ings and enrichments of the urban fabric of the city of Kassel. Behind an exterior that blends the concepts of farm and factory, the interior is finished in laminated wood with skylighting and intense colors; the feeling conveyed is of an intimate interior sheltered by the rugged and neutral exterior.

While it is not a workshop in the strict sense of the word, and also not quite a warehouse, the Miralles-Tagliabue office embodies the idea of a space for building, for experimentation, and for creative work. Wooden cases are used as the library, and old packing cases become tables. The drafting room permits the coexistence of some indigenous furnishings with prototypes executed by the architects themselves. Similarly, old inscriptions and murals that keep appearing from beneath layers of old paint mingle with the designers' patches of color, lamps, tables, and chairs of anonymous authorship. The models and large photomontages serve as adornment, as does also the building's own history, told by the peeling of its walls. A lighted patio relieves the shadows cast from solid walls. Outside, cats sun themselves among the debris of abandoned or discarded models.

The composition of Ricardo Legorreta's office, far from the center of Mexico City and built along a steep hillside, is in the tradition of the ancient Great Hall of a uni-

Robert Delaunay, *Philipe Soupault*, 1922

Henri Matisse, *Violinist at the Window*, 1918

versity. The stairstepped distribution of space affords individuals some privacy, without forcing them to be totally isolated from fellow workers. Tadao Ando also opted for a communal layout in his office in Osaka. Ando's architects work around the circumference of a central patio, roofed in and encircled by tiers extending the full height of the structure.

The Home Office

In an era where technology is being applied toward the liberation of mankind, people are returning home. The electronic age has rendered the visual status of buildings less important, and the home environment has simply become more convenient and often more hospitable to clients. In this way, an intermediate between club and hotel, between the serious place of business and a relaxed space for receiving visitors, has evolved. The importance of clients is weighed by the attention accorded them and by the level of intimacy to which they are privileged. As technology miniaturizes inventions and accelerates the movement of information, it becomes economical and expedient for professionals to work out of a single space, the one in which they reside.

Oscar Tusquets lives on a ground floor surrounded by a garden visible from his studio. The combination of professional with residential space in his case reflects the economy and efficiency of an integrated space; here the architect can design, draw, read, cook, and live—all on a limited budget. The ground-floor dwelling and three additional levels comprise this Catalan designer's tailored premises, his made-to-order environment. There are two separate entrances, the broader and more neutral for clients and suppliers, and the more modest and private for access to the dwelling. The interaction between people and spaces is quite natural; there is a place for everything, and everything is in its place. Internal traffic is likewise differentiated, giving the architect the opportunity to withdraw and think his thoughts undisturbed.

Shoei Yoh and his family lived in an open space, a transparent envelope that laid the expanse and the turmoil of Tokyo at the architect's feet. This transparent dwelling formed the basis of the architect's work; the studio was later walled up following the departure of his children, when Yoh and his wife once more became the nuclear couple. The household was diminished, but the studio flourished and grew. What had been a transparent residence became a diaphanous office, and the opaque basement where the architect had done his designing was remodeled to accommodate conferences and for the storage of written information. Thus in Yoh's case the base office, the reclusive workspace, has been gradually opening to the light, while the dwelling that shared its space has been shrinking.

Ricardo Bofill's Barcelona space occupies the ruins of an old cement plant. This is an atypical case of the professional home office. The two functions are clearly differentiated, sharing only the parking area and the outer access to the complex. In contrasting volumes, the two functions respect and celebrate the mysterious geometry of the original factory, which has a few mixed-use common areas such as the interior patios, the garden, and the main exhibition hall, where the architect makes presentations and holds parties for his guests.

Norman Foster lives at the top of the building he designed to accommodate his London office. On the banks of the Thames, Foster's studio does not seem very residential. It faithfully represents the British architect's design priorities: economy of architectonic idiom, use of contemporary materials, clean treatment of open spaces. These do not include individualization of a building by extraneous criteria. Foster's architecture above all else is his brain child, and it matters little that his studio is located in the same structure as his living quarters. The offices of Foster & Associates serve as the calling card of his enterprise.

To his eclectic dwelling Oswald Mathias Ungers recently added a perfect cube to

Le Corbusier, Ozenfant's house, Paris, 1922

Van Eesteren and Van Doesburg preparing the model of "The Artist's House" for the Rosenberg Exhibition in Paris, 1923

David Teniers, *Archduke Leopold's Collection*, 1635

house his library. The cube in the garden expands the architect's studio and his formal archives. A treasure house in the garden and an architecture gallery of works found on the premises constitute other elements of the bibliophile owner's collections.

Michael Graves' office in a residential section of Princeton, New Jersey, has the features of a domestic space even though it is not one. The architect wished to maintain the residential scale, limiting the size of offices and conference rooms, and reserving the larger spaces for more collaborative kinds of work. The furniture in his work space is characteristically residential, avoiding the standardization that is more common in the office.

A space originally used as a residence is occupied by Mecanoo, who set their architectural office in a distinctive palatial frame. The history of the occupancy of this building is reflected in the successive alterations and additions it has undergone in the years since its construction in 1750. A group of architects and designers acquired the palace in 1970. This initiative—the rehabilitation and remodeling of a structure to serve creative purposes—was a collaboration born of the architects Zaha Hadid, Richard Rogers, Alvaro Siza, and Enric Miralles. After the spaces had been divided among the several studios, Mecanoo took possession of its share in 1995, retaining

the peculiar ornamentation so alien to the architectonic output of the Dutch designers.

Facing the port of Sydney, the Australian architect Harry Seidler erected an office building according to the canons of the International Style. Two of the floors, fronted by a reception area, are occupied by his own offices. Over time, the architect has added open space and a penthouse apartment to accomodate visits from clients and friends.

Warehouse and Loft Offices

The trend of occupying lofts or former warehouses began in the seventies, when a succession of professionals, usually because space was so expensive in the city centers, moved their offices and living quarters into premises on the outskirts that were previously used for storage. Old factories, hangars, and abandoned sheds were thus converted into a new type of housing and commercial space, popular because of the opportunities offered by large, open interiors. The lofts are another intermediate between the workshop and the artist's office. Today, this kind of space is no longer associated with low budgets. Tribeca, located in downtown Manhattan, has been converted from a warehouse neighborhood to a fashionable area with restaurants and other leisure establishments.

Such recycling of industrial architecture has given rise to many architecture

offices. Vittorio Gregotti established his office in a neoclassical building that was once the headquarters of a ceramics manufacturer. In the spirit of an ancient cloister, the architect designed a new gallery and reserved the larger spaces for group work. With the use of glass screens, the geometry accommodated combined facilities for activities, projects, and meetings in a way that avoids any feeling of claustrophobia or remoteness from the scene.

Zaha Hadid and Richard Rogers' offices, both in London, reclaim the notion of the warehouse as a creative space in which order is personal, and the image of order is not a primary condition in the organization of the space. Also in London, Terry Farrell took over a massive mechanical aircraft parts factory built early in the century. Since 1980, Venturi, Scott-Brown and Associates have occupied the whole of a four-story plant in an industrial mill section of Manayunk, near Philadelphia. High roofs, large windows, ample space, and flexibile distribution convinced the architects that the best designer's office would be an industrial loft. Warehouses and old factories were formerly the offices of Richard Meier, Robert Stern, and Gwathmey Siegel, all in Manhattan, although the formal arrangement is more functional in the case of Meier and of Gwathmey Siegel and more ornamental and hierarchical in that of Robert Stern.

Donald Judd's studio

Van de Velde's portable studio in
Brussels, c. 1897

In Santa Monica, California, close by the sea, the Morphosis studio occupies a former plastics factory, its brick structure reinforced with stainless steel. Morphosis saw the studio as a living tool, to be altered and reevaluated by current projects, the true protagonists in the drama of an architectural studio. Also in Santa Monica, Frank Gehry took over a former warehouse for his office. Remodeled and reconstructed by the architect, the former industrial building was subsequently furnished with pieces designed by him.

Jean Nouvel occupies a seventeenth-century building, the former residence of the Duke of Angoulême, at the head of a blind alley in central Paris. Generous spatial dimensions and economy of movement were used to advantage in Nouvel's alterations. He is an outstanding example of the peripatetic architect. Besides having built in many countries of the world, in twenty-five years of professional practice he has repeatedly changed locations as well as partners. Something of this perpetual motion may be seen in the formal variety of his architectonic creations.

The offices of the SITE group of architects in New York occupy an open floor of the Bayard Building, the only example of Louis Sullivan's architecture to be found in the city. The terra cotta ornament of the old warehouse façade evokes the industrial origin of this turn-of-the-century structure.

Frames and moldings, ornamental relics of the past, are painted white, in acceptance of the past without violating the transparency of the present. Like with Richard Rogers and Zaha Hadid, SITE's warehouse space exhibits and celebrates its history.

Buildings with a Past

Among the shops and offices presented here, a unique specimen is the Barcelona building that houses Enric Miralles and Benedetta Tagliabue's offices. It is late-Gothic, the patina of its walls enriched by the vicissitudes of successive uses. In restoring the space, the architects preserved those remnants of the past that harmonize with their latest alterations.

Zaha Hadid located her office in the master's hall of a former London college. The school was built in 1870 over the open pavement of the playgrounds of an Augustinian convent. Traces of the past survive in the structure and façades, which have been left unaltered. Access to the architect's work space is still marked by the inscription "Boys' Entrance," and, ascending to the main floor, one senses the history of the school in the broad, open space.

The origins of the farmhouse in which Michael Graves established his Princeton office date back to the eighteenth century. The building is one of the architectural features of the town's historic tours.

The building occupied by the deconstructionist firm Coop Himmelblau also has historical bloodlines. The office is on the main floor of a late-nineteenth-century building designed by Fellner & Helmer, who executed so many commissions for the Austro-Hungarian monarchy. Since they took possession in 1975, the present owners have acted on several occasions to change finishes and installations, enlarge work areas, or convert them to new uses.

Josef Paul Kleihues works out of a refuse disposal plant, as if to make an ironic statement. This architect is known above all for his work in urban planning, yet his chosen workplace is a former graveyard for wastes, on the river and outside the city of Berlin. In London, likewise on the river, Richard Rogers located his studio in an industrial building of solid civil architecture, recyclable and reclassifiable.

The Architect's Image

The building occupied by Renzo Piano's offices near Genoa embodies his design ideas. Clinging to a hillside, enveloped in greenery, and looking out at the sea, the studio explores possible applications of structures made of fibrous plants and other organic materials. The most characteristic features of the design are its delicate structure and crystal paneling. The architect's predilection for visual and structural lightness is carried to an extreme in

Raoul Dufy, *The Studio on Guelma Street,* 1942

Raoul Dufy, *Studio with Flowers,* 1942

his own work space, permeated by sunlight and vegetation, and in such close touch with the exterior that to those who work there it seems like a pergola. Little by little, Piano's architecture has been finding its own balance between nature and the technology displayed in his earlier works.

A new typology that combines factory and office, the industrial hotel, is a "smart" building designed to accept many and varied activities. Harbored among its tenants is Dominique Perrault, who intended the Berlier Building to be a living system, possessing a transparent body through which its inner life could be seen. The clarity of form and brilliance of materials contrast with the dense, chaotic context of the periphery of Paris. In the interior, the open spaces, the surfaces and materials chosen with a view to convenient maintenance, and the industrial arrangement of functional furnishings and fixtures suggest a technological reinterpretation of earlier utilitarian architecture.

Alexandre Chemetoff insists on the idea of creating "an experimental garden." The architect puts the question in terms of territoriality: rather than disguise the remnants of earlier occupancy, demolish them or simply accept them as they are, the new building should invest them, superimpose itself on them as one more historical stratum, not in terms of the history of a building but in the history of a territory.

Jean-Michel Wilmotte located his office in a traditional neighborhood of cabinetmakers as a statement of his view of the practice of architecture. His office brings together designers, writers, and illustrators of many different nationalities, backgrounds, and cultures in the service of a total architecture, one in which the designer attends to every single detail. Besides architectural projects, Wilmotte's associates design the furniture for his offices. The products designed by the Wilmotte group are for sale on the ground floor, open and lighted as a showroom and visisble from the outside.

Architects whose buildings house independent colleagues—generally designers, architects, or photographers—include Zaha Hadid, Arata Isozaki, Richard Rogers, SITE, and Alvaro Siza. Isozaki shares his space with a photographer, who actually collaborated with the architect to create the work space. Alvaro Siza's building is occupied by several Portuguese architects— Távora, Souto de Moura, and Cavaca—and serves as a singular concentration of Oporto's architectural talents.

With the very traditional intention of conveying a coherent image, Yves Lion and his partner Alain Levitt created offices that are conducive to both reflection and practical work, at once evoking the balance and stability characteristic of their work.

The Taller de Arquitectura of Agustín Hernández in Mexico City was likewise designed to reflect his personal reinterpretation of the organic, by literally emulating and imitating natural growth, with communication between inside and outside. Hernández achieves such communication by repeating the whiteness of his office interior on the exterior surfaces.

Mario Botta placed his studio at the top of a building of his own design, erected in Lugano, a location privileged in the views it affords. Imposing and thoroughly representative of Botta's style, with its solid cylindrical presence, this workshop-office becomes the architect's calling card, a unique recapitulation of his priorities.

Michael Hopkins is another member of the profession who projects the image of his work through the office where it is performed. The tent-like configuration of the roof of his London studio was installed in 1994, when the architect had already adopted similar solutions for certain of his projects, notably the Mound Stand (1987) at Lord's Cricket Ground, the Fleet Velmead children's school (1986), and the first phase of the Schlumberger Research Center (1985).

Nicholas Grimshaw's offices, when seen in abundant natural light from the outside, are visibly connected on several levels by a stairway. This street view is yet another display of the architect's virtuosity.

Balthus, The Artist and his Model, *1981*

Offices of the Future

The architecture most representative of the twentieth century has been that of office buildings, yet offices have changed little from the original models of the early nineteenth century. Function, spatial and budget economy, maximum flexibility and utilization of floor space, and the theoretical statement made by a building have been the chief criteria for construction and arrangement.

The reduction in size and cost of electronic equipment led Peter Drucker to write, in 1992, that commuting to work was becoming obsolete, and that thenceforward it would be feasible to do what seemed impossible in the nineteenth century, namely to move the information, to bring the office to the office worker. The ability to choose the place where a job is to be done will of course change the form of the job, and this new mode of operation requires a space in which, for the designer Francis Duffy, "the workshop idea, the domestic feeling, academic seriousness, market concerns, and hotel-like convenience will have to be combined. The new workplace will have to be convenient, handsome, and practical at the same time." According to Duffy's priorities, the location of the space will become less important. At present, this prospect is confirmed by the success of "business parks" where workers are protected from urban anxieties and tensions, and are surrounded by nature.

Offices have apparently become a litmus test for the changes that living spaces and lifestyles will undergo during the information age. The dematerialization of administrative processes could convert offices from long rows of desks to networks between data centers. Architecturally, this implies a typological change in office buildings. Centralization is no longer of the utmost importance. Work, in many cases, has come to reclaim residential space.

This homecoming, dispensing with papers and filing cabinets, might suggest a kind of utopia, a new practice of working in the street, as witnessed by the widespread use of cellular telephones. Welcome the paperless office, the portable office, the home office. The fluid movement of information and labor noted by Drucker will modify many new homes, in which people will coexist with a new type of work space. The information age is still considered somewhat utopian today, yet even its partial realization, in addition to changes in modes of production, will impact education and cultural affairs. The decline of judgment by appearances, closely linked to the Western importance of visual perception, should lead to other values and criteria, not easy to assimilate after years of what seems like an innate pattern of behavior.

That the development of different channels of communication, and consequently of the distribution of products and sharing of ideas, will open up offices and diversify their locations may seem obvious. However, it falls to the architect—through the design of his own workshop, studio, office, or place of business—to suggest and realize prototype work spaces for the future. In moving to their residences, domesticating their installations, recycling other types of space, or giving priority to social concerns, the architect's workshops, studios, and offices collected in this book seek to point the way toward a possible reconsideration of the workplace.

Anatxu Zabalbeascoa
Barcelona, 1996

Tadao Ando
Kita, Osaka, 1991

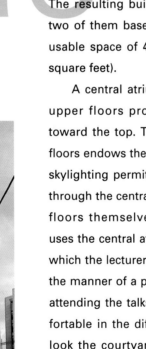

On an irregular plot of 115 square meters (1238 square feet), Tadao Ando wanted to create an expansive and well-illuminated space where he could locate his studio. The resulting building has seven stories, two of them basement floors, and a total usable space of 450 square meters (4842 square feet).

A central atrium that crosses the five upper floors progressively widens out toward the top. The setback of the upper floors endows the space with great vitality; skylighting permits multiple plays of light through the central "courtyard" and on the floors themselves. Occasionally, Ando uses the central atrium as a lecture hall, in which the lecturer employs the staircase in the manner of a podium or a pulpit. Those attending the talks make themselves comfortable in the different spaces that overlook the courtyard, like balconies. Aside from providing natural lighting through all the floors, the atrium lends character to the workplace, fosters the relationship of the design team, and expands communication among employees.

A large library solidly covers one side of the atrium on its ascent through the successive floors. The bookcases lining the wall contrast with the stark power of the reinforced concrete structure.

As demonstrated in his studio, light is an inalienable part of the architect's palette; likewise, the sheer planes of exposed concrete represent a fundamental characteristic of Ando's work.

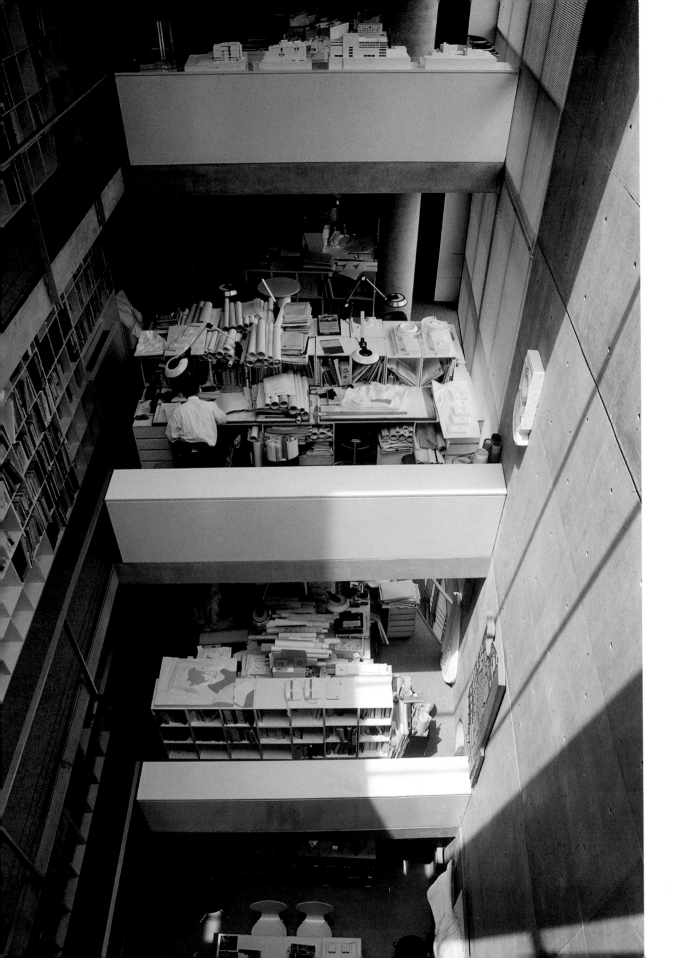
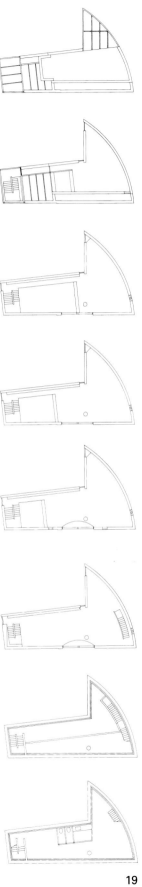

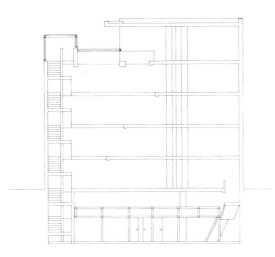

Baufrösche
Kassel, 1993

The Baufrösche (Building Frogs) group consists of seven German architects whose work combines craftsmanship and technology. In constructing their studio in a rural area near Kassel, the designers' collective sought to create a structure that was closer to a workshop than an office building. As such, the new construction fits into its rustic surroundings, and reflects an artistic bent Baufrösche considers more in tune with their brand of architecture.

The three-story building is configured as two rectangular wings, abutted on their long sides and slightly jogged. This is a light prefabricated structure, erected on a sandstone foundation and clad with sheet aluminum and wood siding. The central area provides the vertical connection through an L-shaped stair, which is lined along the last flight with built-in bookcases. Another emergency stair, required by local code, is attached to the back of the building.

The interior contains a succession of spaces, textures, and colors. Its sense of diversity is aided by contrasts set up in the palette: the ochre tones of the furniture and the beech and plywood finishes play against the intense blue of the surfaces, the white of the walls, and the roughness of the facing concrete. Linoleum silences traffic on the concrete floor.

The reception area at the entrance is relatively confined; it has a small window that swivels outward, like all the operable windows in the building. Another glazed opening in the entrance space connects to the adjacent stairwell, drawing additional daylight from the brighter, more generously fenestrated second floor, where many of the drafting tables are located.

The main beechwood stair originates by the studio library and culminates on the third floor in a luminous space that straddles both naves of the building. Minimal partitioning in this room allows the structure to reveal itself in elements reminiscent of the stanchions and shrouds of a sailing vessel. It's an apt association for the studio of a design firm that wishes to signal its dual emphases on craft and engineering.

With a structure that fits its rustic surroundings, the German group's studio is more like a workshop than an office.

A space used as a library (including a browser's seat mounted on the incline) occupies the stairway on its last flight. The stairwell is the central element joining the two jogged halves of the building.

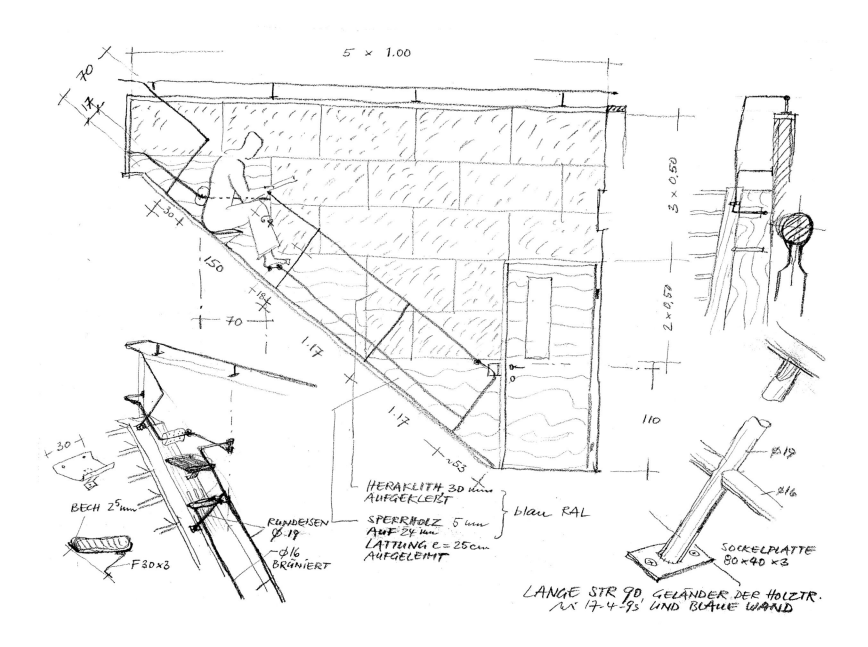

5 × 1.00

70

17

3 × 0.50

2 × 0.50

30

150

184

70

1.17

1.17

53

110

BECH 2⁵ mm

30

F 30 × 3

RUNDEISEN
Ø 19

Ø 16
BRÜNIERT

HERAKLITH 30 mm
AUFGEKLEBT

SPERRHOLZ 5 mm
AUF 24 mm
LATTUNG e = 25 cm
AUFGELEIMT

blau RAL

Ø 19

Ø 16

SOCKELPLATTE
80 × 40 × 3

LANGE STR 90, GELÄNDER DER HOLZTR.
17-4-95 UND BLAUE WAND

24

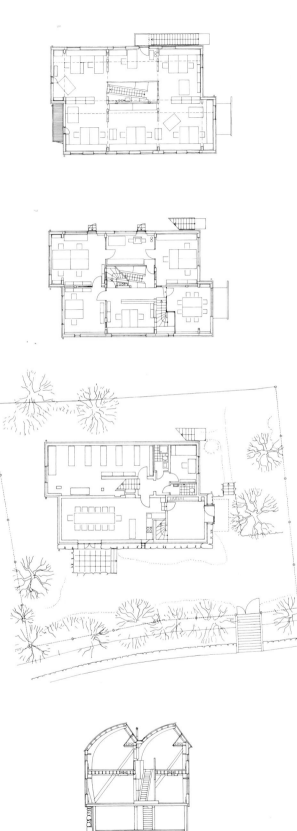

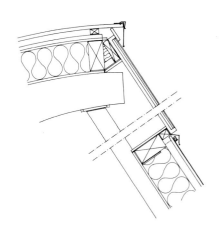

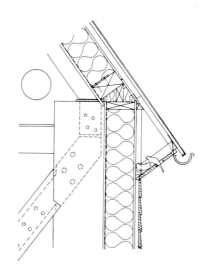

Ricardo Bofill
Sant Just Desvern, Barcelona, 1973–1975

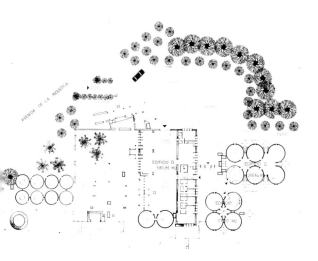

The studio was built amid the silos of a turn-of-the-century factory.

In the early 1970s Ricardo Bofill discovered, very close to Barcelona, a cement factory in disrepair. Its great dimensions gave the structure an air halfway between surreal and crude. The sculptural qualities of the building prompted the Catalan architect to purchase and renovate it to serve a dual function as his architecture workshop, the Taller de Arquitectura, and his residence.

Remodeling the turn-of-the-century factory, comprising more than 30 silos, underground passages, and enormous machine rooms, took almost two years. The rigid structural members that enveloped it were demolished, and tons of cement encroaching on everything were removed, until the final spaces were exposed. Narrow windows were opened in the silo walls, evoking those of Roman structures. A landscaping project was then carried out: the grounds, largely covered with grass, are delimited by groups of eucalyptus, palm, olive, plum, and mimosa trees. An abundance of climbing plants, cloaking the concrete façades, gives the building the mysterious aspect of a romantic ruin.

The Taller de Arquitectura has eight floors of different sizes, dispersed among the silos to accommodate offices, a model workshop, file rooms, a library, and a projection room. The complex has a large central space, christened the "Cathedral," owing to its monumental character. Concerts, exhibitions, and other cultural events associated with the architect's professional activity are held there.

Bofill felt that close contact with the exterior would foster an atmosphere between ruin and cloister, creating for his studio a setting conducive to reflection.

The studio volumes emulate those of the original silos.

The building, circular in plan, measures 25 meters (82 feet) in diameter.

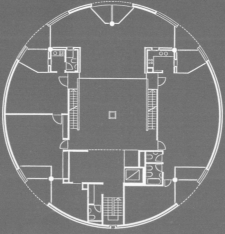

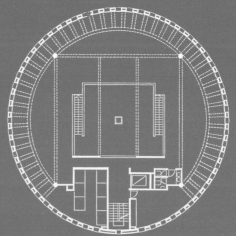

Mario Botta
Lugano, Ticino, 1990

On the outskirts of Lugano, a circular building designed by Mario Botta for himself houses the architect's office. The cylindrical structure, 25 meters (82 feet) in diameter, stands out as a landmark, contrasting with the straight-edged single-family houses lining both sides of the streets surrounding the building.

Botta devised a plan that stacked ground-floor shops, offices, and apartments, with his own studio occupying the privileged top stories crowning the edifice. In choosing to move to a mixed-use building, the Swiss architect sought an environment in which diverse relationships between the architecture and users would lend vitality to the space where he works.

The structure of the building is reinforced concrete lined with facework. The roof, a barrel vault, is insulated with copper panels. The interior walls are plastered and painted white. The studio floor is parquet interspersed with granite slabs that mark the access to the central atrium.

Acting as his own client gave the architect greater room for typological experimentation, evident in the realization of a circular plan and in the customization of his own workstation.

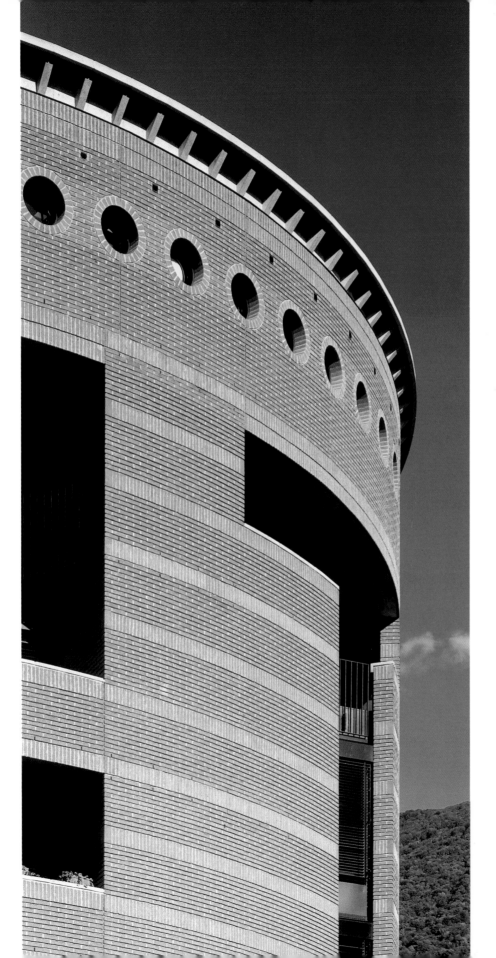
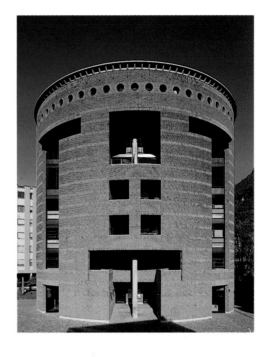
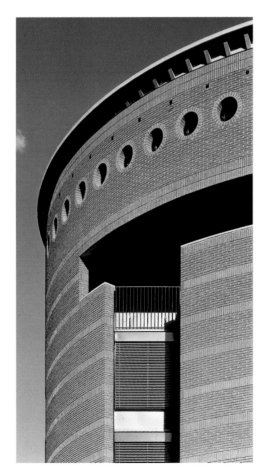

Botta himself occupies the top floor of the building, which was constructed in reinforced concrete with brick cladding.

The barrel-vaulted roof was insulated with copper panels.

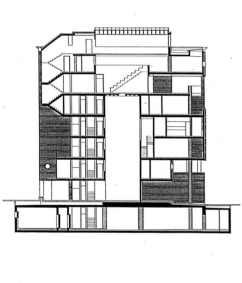

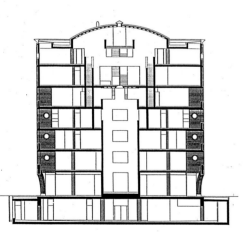

Coop Himmelblau
Vienna, 1975

In the heart of Vienna's historic center, near the Staatsoper, is the studio of Coop Himmelblau. The architects' office occupies the first floor of the Residenzclub House, designed by Fellner & Helmer, a characteristic neoclassical building of Vienna circa 1896. Opposite their office is the historic Variété Ronacher (also by Fellner & Helmer), which is the site of Coop Himmelblau's unrealized, yet renowned project for the rehabilitation of the old theater as a latter-day cultural center.

In 1975 Coop Himmelblau moved into the building and began a gradual conversion of the residential space. Initially, the architects occupied three rooms while they altered finishes and installations to facilitate further phases. They covered an existing gallery with a metal structure and put in wood flooring to accommodate the drafting area. In the final stage they allotted the rooms that the forty-member firm uses at present (an administrative office, two conference rooms, four design areas, a studio, two model workshops, a darkroom, a mailroom, and storage).

The furniture and lighting (drafting tables made of boards on trestles, office chairs with reclining seats, ambient fluorescent lighting, and adjustable table lamps) were planned for efficiency and flexibility, to be deployed as needed for different projects.

There is an ad hoc quality to the architects' office that is very much in keeping with their philosophy: in numerous projects (including the Ronacher Theater) Coop Himmelblau has propounded a "parasitic architecture," in which "found" spaces in existing structures are re-inhabited, and thus reinvented, or transformed.

The Austrian group has another office in Culver City, California.

The studio is located in the center of Vienna's historic district. The neoclassical building has been gradually retrofitted by the architects.

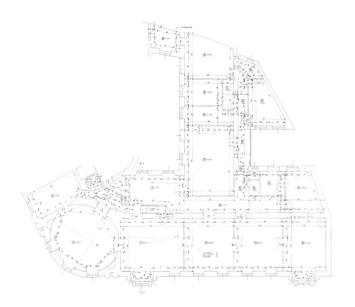

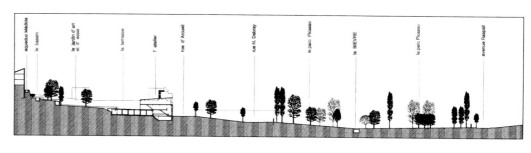

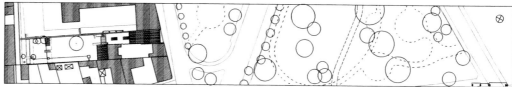

Alexandre Chemetoff
Gentilly, Paris, 1995

In the valley of the Bièvre, a tributary of the Seine near Paris, atop the ancient foundations of various buildings, stands the studio of French architect Alexandre Chemetoff.

The plot occupies a slope between the former course of the Bièvre, covered since the 1960s, at the low end of the site, and the Medici aqueduct at the upper boundary of the property. Constructing the architect's workshop entailed the remodeling of an old house that was sandwiched between the walls of existing structures, its foundations rooted in an old travertine quarry. The conversion presented challenges both structural and contextual. Gutting the existing house revealed that its bearing walls and foundations were bonded to the exterior lot-line walls. Further excavation in the cellar uncovered the remains of what might have been another previous residence.

The successive discoveries prompted Chemetoff to decide to use the entire property and to alter the plan for his studio: the site is a palimpsest of sorts, and rather than disguise, destroy, or simply coexist with the debris of previous structures, Chemetoff's building incorporates the historic fragments, with new additions superimposed on the site like one more layer in the history of a territory.

The building, comprising three stories and a basement, combines reinforced concrete and metal structures. The roofs are of stainless steel, with wood ceilings between floors. The flooring is parquet set in wide pieces of unpolished wood. Except for the Thonet chairs and some wicker pieces in the studio's public areas, the furniture is utilitarian: drafting tables on trestles.

In designing his own studio, Chemetoff emphasized the idea of creating a domain he now defines as an experimental garden.

The building rises on a mild slope between the old course of the Bièvre river and an aqueduct. Chemetoff refers to his studio as an "experimental garden."

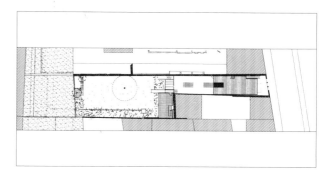

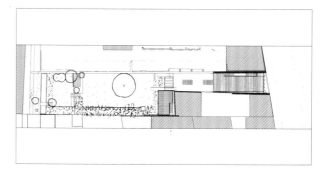

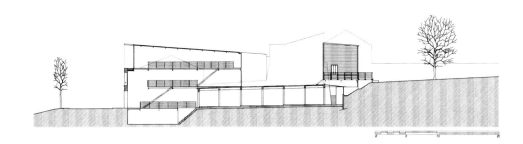

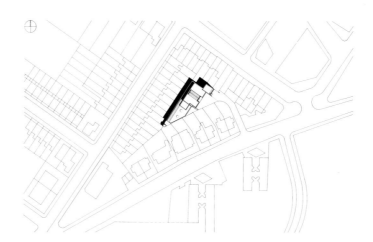

Site plan: the studio as urban infill.

David Chipperfield
London, 1989

The front doors to the dual studios.

David Chipperfield's studio occupies a residual triangular plot in the center of a wedge-shaped block in the northern Camden Town district of London. Because of its exposure to surrounding residences, its lack of frontage on the main street, and its single access, the property was used for many years as a furniture warehouse. As if it were a collective attic, obsolete merchandise and the useless junk of the whole community accumulated there.

To address the lack of privacy, Chipperfield designed a largely enclosed structure with skylights and a highly flexible interior layout, similar to a loft building. The architect reinforced the loft or warehouse character of the Camden Town studio with the austerity and hardness of the materials he decided to use. The front of the office building consists of an entrance porch flanked by symmetrical steel and glass block walls. The separation between the two studios occupying the space is expressed on the façade by a pair of translucent side lights and a protruding concrete fin that forms the partition bifurcating the interior. Skylights flood the building with light through openings between the floors. The pale concrete walls and translucent entrance façade contribute to the distribution of daylight. As in most of his projects, the British architect's studio was furnished with close attention to the functional, minimalist character of the furniture.

Although introversion was an idea frequently used by architects of the Victorian era when building artists' studios, it is likely that Chipperfield's inspiration came from elsewhere: his control of the studio's environment and views (the upper level of the building has no windows and is lighted exclusively from above) is a direct reference to traditional Japanese architecture, which promotes an atmosphere of calm. In the late 1980s, when Chipperfield built his studio, the architect was beginning to pattern his plans after that oriental vernacular, which subsequently had great importance in the development of his career.

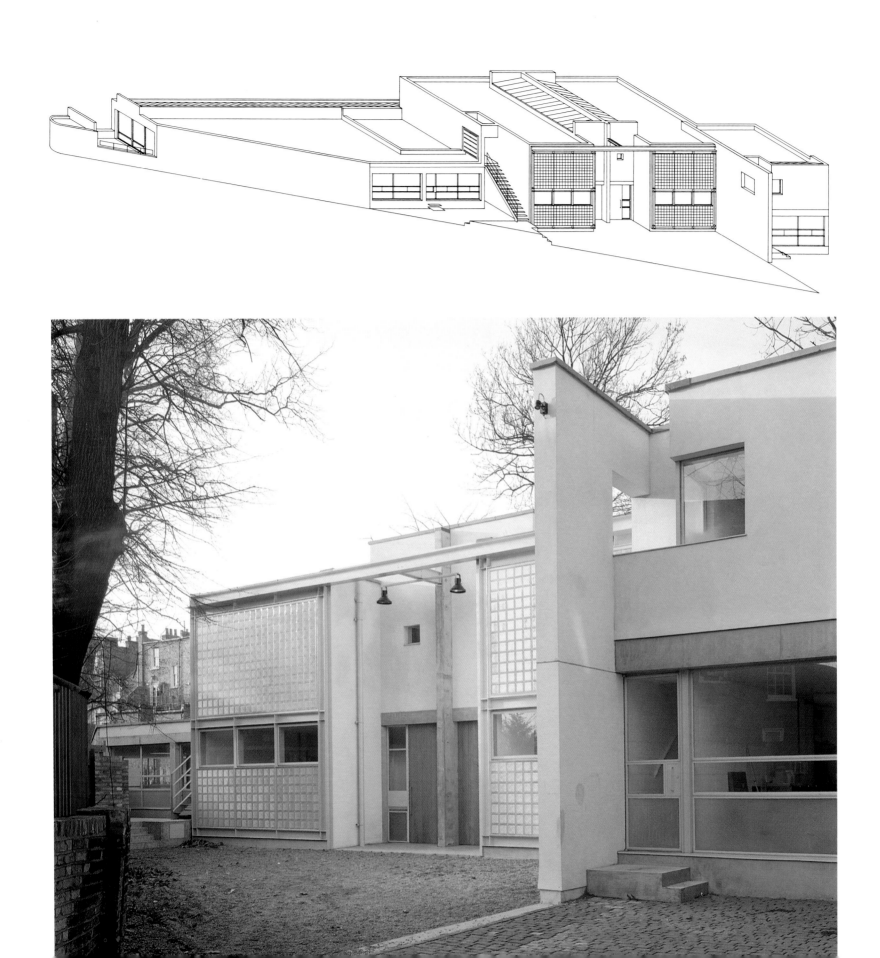

The pared-down furnishings are characteristic of Chipperfield's work.

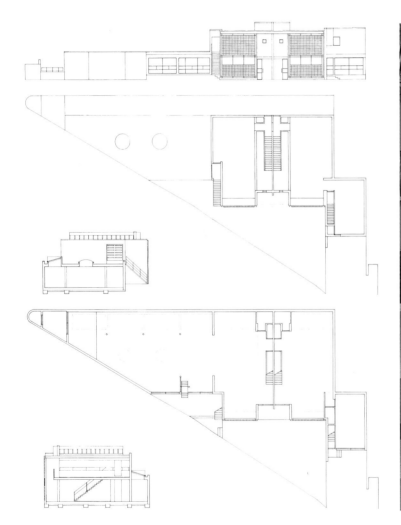

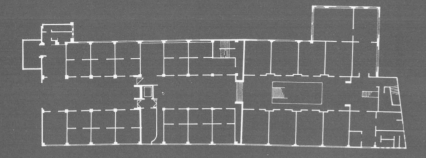

farrell

Terry Farrell
London, 1987

The architect's studio occupies an old factory in London's Edgware Road district.

In the late 1980s a lack of space compelled the group of architects headed by Terry Farrell to move to an old factory in the Edgware Road district of London.

The building was constructed in 1920 to accommodate the production line of the Bovis Company, a manufacturer of household furniture. In 1940 the demands of war led to a change in production, when the facilities were converted to the manufacture of parts for aircraft repair and replacement.

Throughout its history, the industrial character of the building made it possible for new occupants to vary its use; when Terry Farrell & Partners undertook to convert the old factory into their offices, they proceeded from two principal architectural decisions: the insertion of a stair, and the creation of a skylighted interior courtyard that runs the length of the building, connecting all the spaces, while giving them access to natural light. The courtyard is now decorated with climbing plants and model airplanes. The offices are concentrated on both sides of the atrium and the work spaces can be isolated by means of a discrete system of rabbeted wood screens covered with fireproof plywood.

Electric power is distributed via outlets around the perimeter. The architects' office is decorated with period pieces such as Biedermeier sofas and Odeon wall lamps of copper and zinc, which illuminate the reception area.

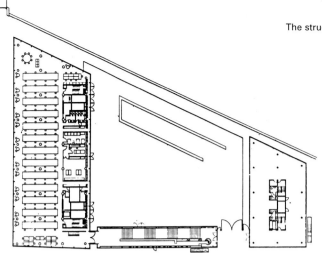

Norman Foster
London, 1990

foster

The firm of Sir Norman Foster and Partners is housed in a building of its own design on the south bank of the Thames, near Battersea Bridge. The eight-story structure contains the architects' offices on the ground, first, and mezzanine levels, thirty apartments on levels three to seven, and two duplex penthouses. A glass canopy links the main building to a two-story glazed pavilion at the rear of the site.

The entrance to the main building is grandly scaled, with a stately, 130-foot-long stair that proceeds from the 26-foot-high entrance to the reception area on the first floor, and beyond it, to the double-height studio overlooking the water. (An elongated bar extending along one side of the stair provides a popular pit stop for employees, and a novel waiting area for guests.)

The main studio itself is outfitted with similar boldness and seeming simplicity: thirteen vast drafting tables (each 36 feet long) are arrayed perpendicular to the great north curtain wall, affording river views to all the workstations. Service and support spaces, including audiovisual

rooms, model shops, and computers, are laid in a band along the south wall. All the mechanical systems are contained under the raised floor, with power, data, and telephone outlets housed in totems under the work surfaces. The mezzanine provides additional flexible work spaces.

The architects' formidable library is arrayed in tall banks of shelves running parallel to the office's rear (south-facing) wall. A narrow ambulatory between the shelves and the building envelope affords unimpeded access to the stacks.

Foster has long been recognized for his holistic approach, marked by his firm's consistent efforts to integrate diverse aspects of architecture and technology, interior and industrial design. Suitably, in this building, the architects designed most of the furnishings and the furniture, down to the exit signs. Various work surfaces and chairs were made by Tecno, the Italian manufacturer for whom Foster has designed several office lines.

Views of the approach to the offices and the bar lining the stair.

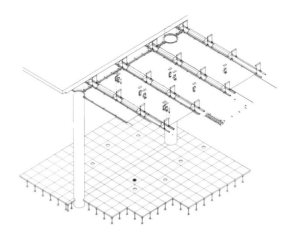

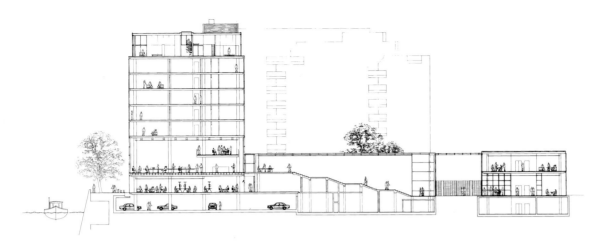

Frank O. Gehry
Santa Monica, California, 1988

gehry

The building was erected in the 1950s for industrial use. The floor plan, top, conflates the street-level lobby and the second-floor studio.

Located one mile from the Pacific Ocean, the Santa Monica office of Frank O. Gehry & Associates is an example of functional architecture. The two-story building, constructed in the 1950s, extends over one whole block in an area of industrial buildings and warehouses, today largely occupied by art galleries and movie producers' offices.

Entered at street level, the corner lobby has a small stair leading to the main floor, which is divided into three distinct zones. The central area is given over to an open studio illuminated by several eccentric skylights. East of the studio, the office is split between two levels that are connected by a stair running along the south wall, within a sizable open well. The lower level (annexed to the office at a later date) holds the library and computerized drafting stations; the main-level galleries lining two sides of the stairwell house an additional work area and, in the northeast corner, the woodworking room and model shop. Here the large pieces of sculpture used for project presentations are produced.

Gehry's own work space, a self-contained office and loft, stands west of the open studio. Large glazed barn doors on the enclosure's north and east walls enable Gehry to open his office to adjacent work areas, essentially "dematerializing" the volume of this small "building within a building." A series of discrete rooms and open offices line the north and west peripheries; the main conference room adjoins the lobby stair.

Most of the flooring and partitions are made of wood and plywood panels. All the furniture, with the exception of the drafting chairs, was designed by Gehry himself. The prototypes of the famous recycled cardboard chairs manufactured by Vitra furnish the architect's office and the conference room.

Far from the sculptural forms characterizing most of his work, Gehry's studio is a straightforward and rational space where lighting and convenience have been among the chief factors determining the layout and the materials used. This is a studio more pragmatic than representative, more functional than showy: notwithstanding its formal disparity, it has a hands-on quality that is entirely consistent with Gehry's architecture.

Gehry's studio is functional rather than ostentatious;
an open well connects the ground-floor studio to the
main design area above.

The double-height well accommodates the large
mock-ups produced by the architect.

Support spaces line the periphery.

The building occupied by the architect's studio has been designated as a historic landmark.

Michael Graves
Princeton, New Jersey, 1982

graves

The offices of Michael Graves are located in one of the most notable buildings in Princeton, New Jersey. Listed in the *National Register of Historic Places*, it consists of two structures, built almost 90 years apart. The original nucleus of the property was constructed in 1750 as a farmhouse, which subsequently underwent numerous expansions and remodelings. The largest of these was the addition of three floors in 1841. The building has been used for various purposes, as a residence, a hotel, and even as a dormitory for students of the Evelyn School, a college that was for years associated with Princeton University, located a few blocks down the street.

The distinctive character and scale of the building were determining factors in Graves's decision to renovate it. In large part, the remodeling entailed a restoration of the building; beyond that, false ceilings were hung to improve the acoustics, and fluorescent fixtures installed by previous owners were removed.

At present, the building comprises a series of rooms on a domestic scale and more spacious public areas for collective work. Several rooms have fireplaces, one of which still retains the original mantel and surround.

The building is decorated throughout with models and drawings by Graves. This display, added to the historic importance of the structure, and the fact that it is a working architect's studio, has made the building on Nassau Street a popular stop on cultural tours of Princeton.

The architect chose a domestic scale and intimacy for his studio.

Vittorio Gregotti
Milan, 1972

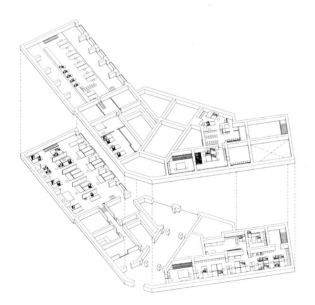

The architectural studio of Gregotti Associati is situated in a building constructed toward the end of the last century by architect Luigi Broggi. The building, commissioned by a family of ceramic artists, was designed in the neoclassical style and decorated with ceramic ornamentation generated by the family enterprise.

The nucleus of Gregotti's studio is located in a wing overlooking the back garden, which was once occupied by the old firing kilns. The wing's five original bays are defined by brick arches spanning the volume, and a corresponding five-bay arcade to the garden. To enclose the openings, Gregotti superimposed a slender framework of steel and glass on the exterior wall, thereby creating a series of delicate bay windows without altering the sense of the original arcade.

In remodeling the interior, the architect took a similar tack, electing to create a freestanding, unambiguously modern insertion that did not violate the existing structure. Four transverse concrete fins, aligned with the arches, were cast along the center axis of the hall. They support a raised rectangular floor that functions as a

mezzanine, with a skeletal stair at one end. The concrete walls define five work areas on ground level, and a corresponding number on the slab above. Large drafting tables are placed in each of these areas, with a view to giving the designers a degree of independence without chopping up the original volume. Ventilation and power delivery is incorporated into the inserted structure.

A large arch connects the entrance hall with a study area where the library and files of the Milan firm are archived. The cafeteria is situated in a cloistered area adjoining the main part of the building.

In 1987 the studio of Gregotti Associati was expanded to occupy the second floor of the old building; the second-phase remodeling followed principles similar to those that shaped the first phase.

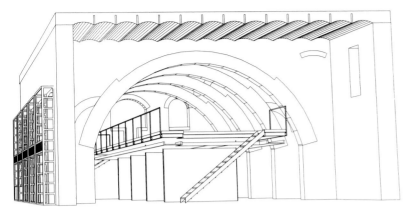

The architect converted an old industrial structure, opening it vertically and horizontally. A new stair became the office centerpiece.

Nicholas Grimshaw
London, 1993

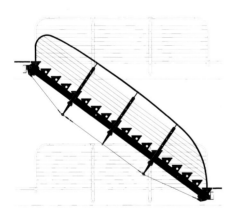

When it became necessary to move his studio, Nicholas Grimshaw decided to remain in the center of London so that he could be close to his consulting engineers and be easily accessible to clients. The six-story building selected by the firm was a former belt factory. It was in an appropriate location and had generous overall dimensions, but the rooms within were confined and poorly illuminated. These drawbacks prompted the architect to give priority to creating well-lit open spaces in remodeling his new office. Grimshaw wanted each of the designers to have enough room to experiment with models and full-scale mock-ups.

The conversion of the building consisted of opening it up vertically and horizontally, and replacing the original structure with another of stainless steel. The new bearing structure permitted the creation of sizable open spaces, capable of accommodating the development of large-scale work. The roof of the building was partially replaced. A skylighted well was opened up for a new staircase and in this way the core of the building was naturally illuminated. The ground-floor façade was also replaced by glass walls, which drew light into the interior. The opened building is now a showcase highlighted by the central stair, demonstrating the components of creative engineering, light structure, prefabrication, and high quality finishes so central to Grimshaw's architecture.

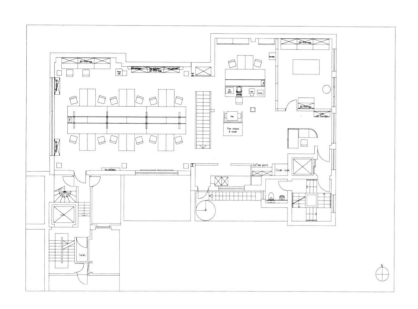

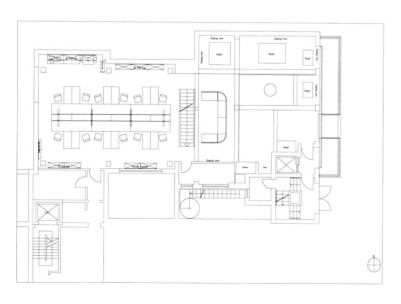

Gwathmey Siegel
New York, 1982

The architects selected an old warehouse in Manhattan as the site for their studio. With the exception of the sprinkler system, the windows, the radiators, and the columns, the space was in poor condition and required substantial refurbishment. The organization of the plan arose from the placement of the large windows, overlooking Tenth Avenue to the east and 36th Street to the south, and the location of the elevators on the west side of the building.

The office was laid out with two peripheral corridors running along the north and south walls. The files and plans of current projects are kept in storage lining the north passage; the south corridor contains firm catalogues, reference materials, three conference rooms, and the material samples library. The freight elevators, occupying the northeast corner, are adjoined by a carpenter's shop, a model shop, and a small kitchen.

Relegating the ancillary functions to the periphery allowed the main work area of the studio to occupy the center of the floor without visual obstructions. It holds forty-eight drafting stations, each semi-enclosed and individually lighted. The conference and presentation rooms, and the offices of the partners, are secluded in a more private area at the east end of the space.

Vertical reference points in the configuration of the old warehouse were used to organize some of the systems for the new offices: the ambient lighting and air conditioning systems were accommodated in the space between the ceiling and the datum line set by the tops of the large windows; the bookcases' height was determined by the maximum height of the windowsills.

Visitors arriving in the elevators encounter a lobby screened by translucent glass doors. The sliding panels open on a reception area and a waiting room-cum-exhibition space that introduces the spatial dynamic of the open warehouse, elegantly rendered with Gwathmey Siegel's characteristic attention to dominant geometries, rhythm, and proportion.

The office comprises forty-eight work stations organized between two peripheral passageways.

Zaha Hadid
London, 1985

The London building housing the Iraqi architect's studio occupies a site that was originally part of the Augustinian convent of St. Mary's. After the great fire of 1666, its landowner, the Earl of Northampton, leased the property until, in 1870, a school was built. When the old Victorian school closed in the mid-1970s, the building was converted into an art center shared by various architecture studios, graphic designers, and photographers. Located in the Farringdon district in the eastern part of the city, the brick building still has two entrances: one for boys and another for girls. Admittance to Hadid's studio is gained through a door emblazoned "Boys' Entrance."

Occupying the first floor of one of the wings, the studio is a 120-square-meter (1290-square-feet) open space that formerly held one of the main classrooms and the teachers' conference room. Hadid removed the flimsy doors that were blocking sightlines and traffic, to create a wide central space in which there are long angular drafting tables designed by the architect herself. A storeroom, a library/conference room, a file area, and a small loft complete the studio. All the employees share the same work space, from the administrative manager to the architect herself.

On top of the white drafting tables, and hanging from the light-colored walls, is a series of models and drawings that turn the studio into a spacious gallery. The vibrantly colored pile carpet was designed by Hadid for the German firm of Vorwerk. The rest of the furniture—bookcases and chairs—is from diverse sources, casually arranged to lend the studio an eclectic air.

The architect's studio occupies the teachers' room of a Victorian school.

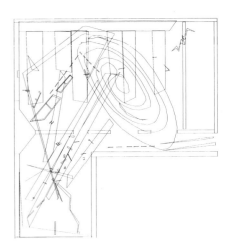

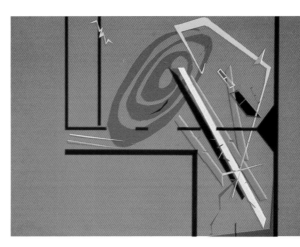

The carpeting in warm colors and the work table were designed by Hadid.

Agustín Hernández
México, D.F., 1972–1995

hernández

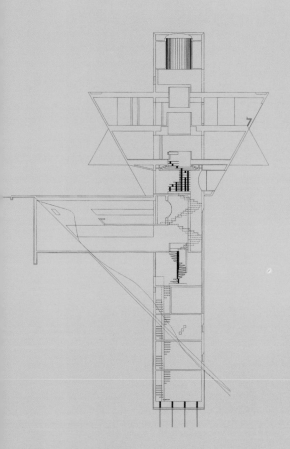

A plot with a 45-degree slope compelled Agustín Hernández to design his studio with an understanding of natural structures. By emulating the organic model of the tree, the Mexican architect was able to minimize his construction's impact on the steep site, while preserving the freedom to create floor plans unfettered by the topography.

On a shaft, or trunk, erected with earthquake-resistant anchors serving the function of roots, four polyhedral volumes, stacked in pairs, constitute the tree "canopy." The upper prismoids are laid at right angles to the lower ones; three pairs of cables, visible on the building exterior, brace the structure. The access bridge serves another purpose as a horizontal brace.

The building is made of reinforced concrete sheathed, in sections, with white marble. The cladding is intended to reveal what is happening inside, where the walls and most of the surfaces are white. The geometry of the interiors, on the other hand, echoes the angular extremes of the outdoor environment.

The fact that Hernández chose a formal solution inspired by an arboreal model reflects his particular view of organic architecture and its connection to the site. Similarly, the design is consistent with the architect's emphasis on creating a dialogue between a building's exterior and interior. The studio amply demonstrates the architect's premise that natural structures can provide keys for new and creative structural solutions.

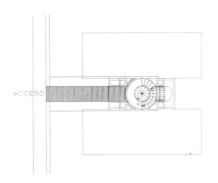

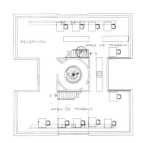

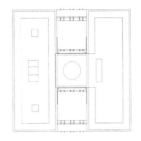

The structure, of reinforced concrete, was designed to resist earthquakes.

Michael Hopkins
London, 1994

Reception area.

Taut canopy structures are typical features of buildings by Michael Hopkins & Partners. Since 1994, the architects' offices in the north end of London have been adorned with a waterproof fabric canopy that unifies the discrete parts of the studio. Shielded by the canopy, the reception area is housed in a transparent rectangular volume based on the model that the architects created for the Victoria and Albert Museum in 1987. It leads to two main wings housing designers and draftspersons, printers, a model shop, storage, a garage, and a small garden.

Aside from its use as a unifying element, the new tensile roof marks the main entrance and provides protection from inclement weather. In addition, it operates in the summer as a gallery for exhibitions, conferences, and other social functions.

The canopy, which is drained at four points, extends along an old brick wall marking the boundary of the property. The wall was reinforced with concrete to support the steel structure that holds up the roof. Characteristically for Hopkins's work, the connection assemblies securing cables and fabric are derived from nautical technology. In assembling the crystalline enclosure for the reception, the architects achieved maximum transparency by using silicone to buttglaze both the glass infill panels and the glass stiffening structure.

The new offices are air-conditioned through floor grates and buried ducts. With the structural loads transferred to the peripheral walls, the mechanical systems hidden, the various lighting systems recessed, and the partitions made of transparent materials, Michael Hopkins's office forms a generously illuminated, uninterrupted space. At nightfall, it casts light like a lantern, in contrast to the daytime, when the building absorbs natural light.

General view of new roof, added in 1994.

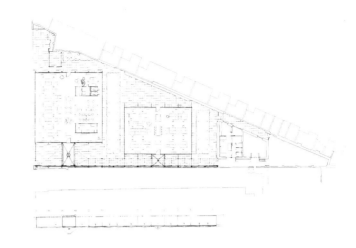

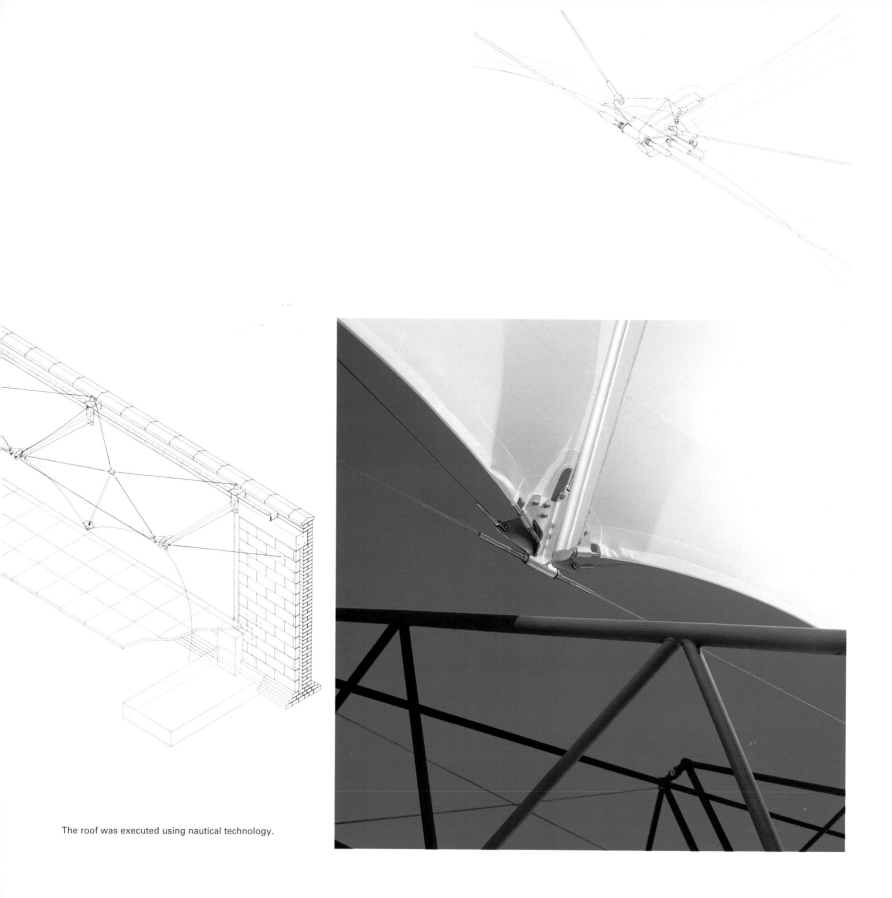

The roof was executed using nautical technology.

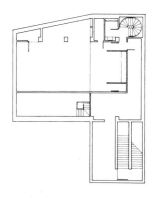

Arata Isozaki
Tokyo, 1985

In Roppongi, one of the most fashionable districts of the Japanese capital, Arata Isozaki designed a concrete building to house his workshop and a photographer's studio. The photographer preferred a space open to the outside, capable of absorbing as much natural light as possible, and yet isolated from the distractions and noises of a large city. For that purpose, the Japanese architect built a courtyard, surrounded by high walls, in the area adjoining the entrance.

In 1991 the architect expanded his own studio, taking over and covering the courtyard with a translucent vaulted structure. It now functions as a workshop for scale models and experimentation with materials. Besides the drafting stations that occupy an entire floor, the studio includes a conference room, an administration and reception area, and Isozaki's own study. The designer's office is a simple, secluded room, a library retreat where Isozaki shuts himself in to concentrate on his designs.

Isozaki still shares his workplace with the photographer, who now occupies the basement and the second floor of the building.

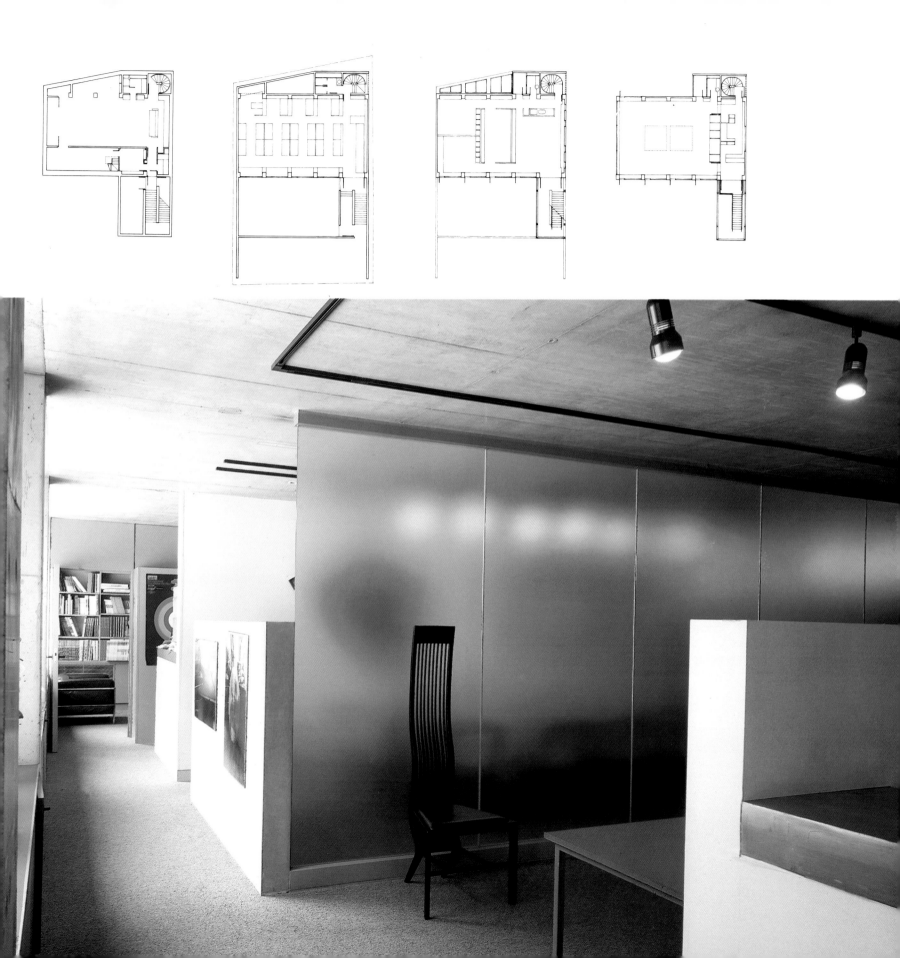

The architect's study retreat.

The architect's model shop occupies the former courtyard, now enclosed by a tentlike structure.

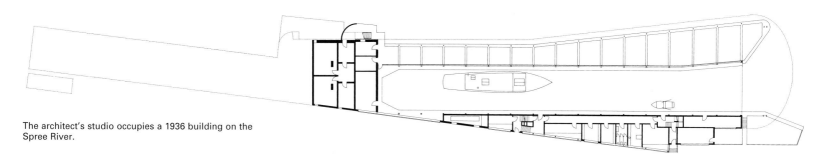

The architect's studio occupies a 1936 building on the Spree River.

Josef Paul Kleihues
Berlin, 1986

The riverfront building occupied since 1986 by the office of Josef Paul Kleihues was built in 1935 as a refuse disposal loading site. Designed by Paul Baumgarten, the original building was constructed with bearing brick and sheet metal walls, and is typical of his rational architecture of that period. When the building fell into disrepair, public health authorities decided to demolish it; Berlin city planning officials dissented, and sought a new tenant for the old industrial structure. Kleihues bought Baumgarten's building and, following municipal guidelines for the rehabilitation of buildings of artistic merit, adapted it to serve as his office.

The building is located on the Spree River. A paved plaza at street level spans a 260-foot pier, one level below. The drafting room occupies the old plant's central space at street level, accommodating thirty-three people dispersed among twenty design stations and a presentation section. On the floor beneath the studio, at pier level, Kleihues adapted diverse spaces to house a model shop, a computer room, file storage, a kitchen, and studio services. The slip itself is now used by the architect as a private mooring.

Kleihues's intervention consisted mainly of restoring the original building. The contemporary Berlin architect bore in mind the principles that guided his admired predecessor, and took pains to preserve the spirit of the original construction. Kleihues's affinity for it is hardly suprising, given his own work's grounding in what he calls "poetic rationalism." Wherever possible, Kleihues maintained the building's proportions, structure, palette, and plan, including distinctive elements such as the heavy wooden doors, and the metal-frame strips used for both windows and opaque paneling.

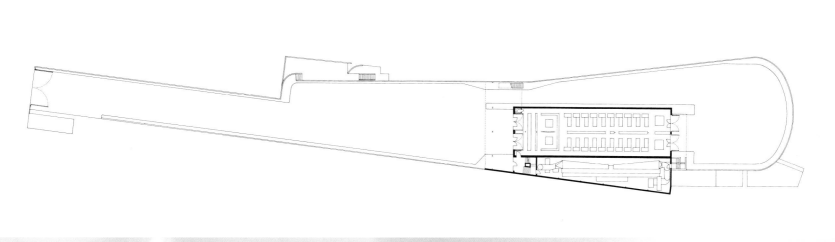

Strip windows and *pilotis*, below, bespeak a Modern lineage.

Kleihues reclaimed the metal frames and heavy wooden doors of the original Baumgarten edifice.

Ricardo Legorreta
México, D.F., 1966

legorreta

The desire to create a functional and restful environment, conducive to creative work, guided the decisions in the design of architect Ricardo Legorreta's studio.

The sloping site, near the limits of Mexico City, offers a panoramic view. Endeavoring to reduce the exposure to traffic, noise, and the stress they produce, Legorreta reinforced the building's sense of privacy and seclusion with his choreography of the approaches to the building. His treatment includes elements characteristic of his work, such as wall planes functioning as solid screens, punched openings, and cascading stairs, which together allow the architect to control the sightlines. Legorreta's construction, by these means, is also intergrated into the landscape, forming a sculptural complex evocative of a plastic arts workshop.

The office contains a reception area (which is also the building's entrance hall), a design studio, and a conference room. The design studio itself is located at the bottom of the building, and is reached via a series of staircases. This drafting area, configured in rising tiers like an amphitheater, affords a general view of the space, while individualizing the work area of each designer.

The interior's massive, roughly textured walls, light-bathed vaulted ceilings, carefully placed small openings, and varying changes in level, render spaces that are plastic, somewhat mysterious, and sensual.

The studio is integrated into a steep hillside.

lion

Yves Lion
Paris, 1990

After a long odyssey that took them through Parisian ateliers and commercial offices, Yves Lion and his partner Alain Levitt decided to plan an efficient building that would provide the best conditions for architectural design, projecting a finely tuned image for the thirty-member firm. Far from being a showcase of architectural flourishes and sophisticated materials, Lion and Levitt's building aims to portray the levelheaded ingenuity that characterizes the spirit of their work.

The site is sandwiched between the lot-line walls of neighboring structures, limiting the exposures of the building to the front and rear façades. Lion designed an eight-story building with floorplates approximately 90 square meters (970 square feet) in area. The conference room and the space set up for presentations and slide projection are located on the top floor, beneath a shallow barrel vault. The floor below accommodates Lion's office, the studio management, and a secretarial station. Both upper floors are set back on two sides, allowing the insertion of skylights that illuminate the design studio on the fourth floor. Levitt's office is on the third floor, along with a boardroom, the documentation center, and administration. The second floor, distinguished by its generous strip windows, houses additional drafting tables. Located on the ground floor are the files, technical services, and the reception area. The basement holds a samples and testing laboratory where scale models are made. The basement draws daylight from a tall, skylighted extension behind the building, which is raised one half-level above basement grade.

White is the predominant color in the interior; the street-facing exterior of the building combines reinforced concrete with white Carrara marble cladding. Similarly spare drafting tables and Thonet chairs furnish a building devoid of any other ornamentation than the play of light.

The architects' pragmatic ingenuity can be seen in the handling of the building section: restricted to two exposures, they deployed relatively simple devices, such as the setbacks and the greenhouse extension, to yield spaces that enjoy abundant natural light. Moreover, the quality and quantity of the light varies from floor to floor, depending on the uses intended for each.

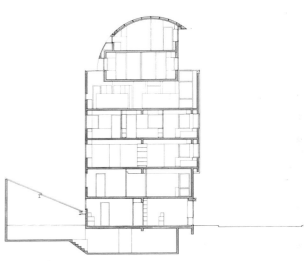

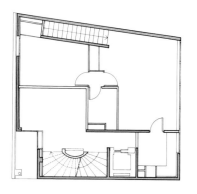
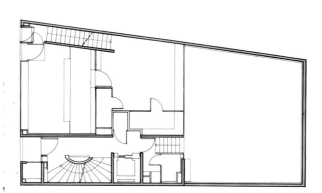
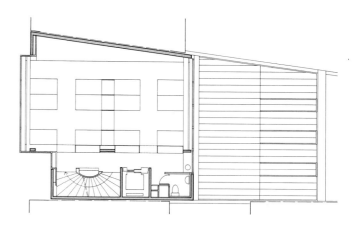

Vaulted conference room on the top floor (above, left).
A skylighted studio (above, right).

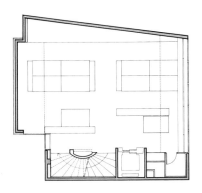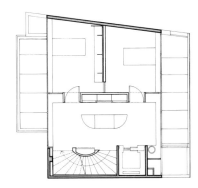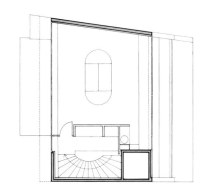

Diverse lighting conditions are available among the design studios.

109

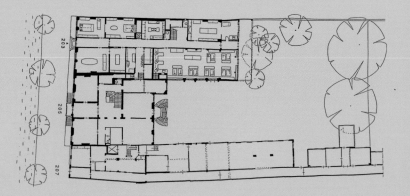

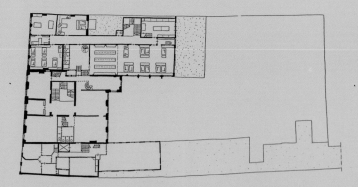

Mecanoo
Delft, 1995

mecanoo

The building occupied by Mecanoo, a group of Dutch architects, has its origins in two dwellings built in the mid-1500s. In 1750 the Italian architect Bollina designed a mansion that joined the two houses, using the former separation between them to form a passageway and a stair. Bollina decorated the ceilings and interior doors with Louis XIV-style moldings, and added a cornice on the street façade. The joining of two dwellings of different sizes, different heights, and different proportions yielded a single structure with numerous spatial quirks.

The picturesque building was occupied over the years by several illustrious tenants. In the mid-nineteenth century it was acquired by the Catholic Church for use as an asylum and an almshouse. When a cholera epidemic broke out a few years later, the mansion was converted into a hospital, which was steadily expanded until it reached the limits of the site. In 1970 a group of architects bought the former hospital and adapted it. Mecanoo acquired part of that space in 1983, and in 1995 set up its office studio there.

It may seem odd to find Mecanoo—known for its distinctly modern idiom—occupying a building so rooted in the past. Further acquaintance with the firm's work, however, resolves that paradox: Mecanoo's Modernism is decidedly nondoctrinaire; far from adhering to a clean-slate approach, the architects relish opportunities to embed their work in an existing context. For instance, a housing complex completed in 1994 in the heart of Maastricht is inserted into the city fabric, and it reconfigures an urban square with subtle consideration for existing connections. Another well-known example is the firm's bank headquarters in Budapest, which combined the careful restoration of a historic building with the addition of an inventive, if not radical, construction on the roof.

This ability to balance the new and the old is brought home in the studio, where the firm consciously kept its interventions to a minimum: new lighting was designed to favor the old moldings, and the furniture was confined to very simple pieces of modest design that did not compete with the visible history of the building.

The ancient building has a motley history.

The latter-day presentation room.

Richard Meier
New York, 1986

meier

In 1986, three years after the firm was founded, Richard Meier & Partners purchased an old warehouse on the West Side of Manhattan. The tall industrial space, about 4000 square feet in area, was blessed with views to the north, south, and east. The remodeling consisted of removing superfluous elements to expose the original structure. The renovation maintained the existing 17-foot-high windows to ensure abundant daylight for the studio.

The end result, a rectangular space with low partitions and few enclosures, allows for flexibility in organizing the teams for diverse projects.

The predominantly white, unobstructed interior, with the mechanical systems neatly sheathed in painted ducts, gives the impression of pristine regularity; the rectilinear, abstract compositions formed by repetitive structural components and the articulation of the built-in furniture, clearly reflect the crisp, controlled design aesthetic of the forty-member firm.

Reception area and model showroom.

Interior space, white and pristine, reflects the
architects' taste.

The studio occupies a building of late-Gothic origin in the center of Barcelona.

miralles

Enric Miralles and Benedetta Tagliabue
Barcelona, 1990

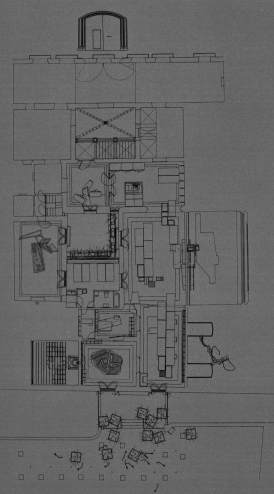

The studio of Enric Miralles and Benedetta Tagliabue is located in a building of late-Gothic origin. Its rear façade was partially renovated in the seventeenth century, and the main façade was repaired within the last 100 years. When the architects discovered the building in 1990, it had been abandoned for more than forty years. Its proprietors were cats that came in through the chimney.

The designers cleaned the building, stripping walls and floors; they uncovered colors, drawings, and inscriptions that had been hidden under generations of paint. On the upper walls of the main space, under the old coating, an original pictorial decoration appeared, which today accompanies the new, variously colored finishes. Stripping the old cornices revealed moldings decorated in gilt and Pompeian red tones.

Furnishing the studio is a never-ending task; elements designed by the architects themselves ("Squashed" chair, "Vacant" bench, and "Unsteady" table) share the space with found pieces. The shelving was built of iron tubing and fastened to the old bearing walls. The sliding doors marking off the spaces are used as partitions and display panels.

Another type of shelving, made of wooden boxes where the slides are arranged, is growing year by year. So is the assortment of furniture and scale models. Ten trees planted over wooden irrigation ducts are thriving, too, protected by prototypes of the pergolas built for Avenida Icaria in Barcelona.

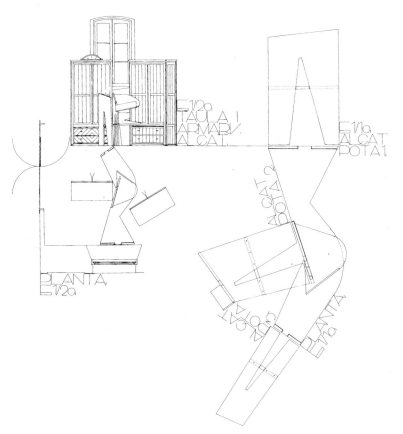

Two interior views of the entrance.

Main drafting and projection area, below.

The conference gallery.

Eclectic furnishings (such as the Arne Jacobsen chairs) contrast with the architecture.

Morphosis
Santa Monica, California, 1993

Since the summer of 1993, the Morphosis studio has occupied an old plastics factory near the Pacific Ocean. It is an industrial structure of exposed brick, whose single-floor layout honors the *atelier* tradition. The exterior, painted in light tones and screened by shrubs and cypresses, retains the sign that used to identify the old factory, giving no clue to the new use of the property. The studio is entered through a service door situated in the rear of the old structure.

Inside, the architects removed the existing partitions, restored the vaulted roof, and polished the original wooden trusses. The floor was raised to accommodate wiring and finished with birch ply panels. The rear (entrance) wall was made to slide, to make it possible to open the studio to the outdoors.

Following the earthquake of January 1994, the original structure was reinforced with a new one of stainless steel, and after the office was computerized, some of the skylights and large windows were covered with shades to limit exposure to the sun.

A white folding screen separates the reception area from the rest of the studio.

The model shop opens on the street, using the old factory loading dock. The files, conference room (with a table of the architects' design), photographic laboratory, kitchen, and bathroom, are gathered at one end of the building, under a loft used for storage.

The tectonic preoccupations of the firm are evident everywhere in the studio: in the attention lavished on the existing structure, the thoughtful juxtapositions of old and new materials, and, most of all, in the detailing of the freestanding shelving, partitions, and lighting.

The interior partitions of the original plastics factory were removed.

The architects retained the old vaulted roof and timber trusses. The original structure was reinforced, after the earthquake of 1994, with new steel seismic bracing.

The seventeenth-century building was formerly a ducal residence.

Jean Nouvel
Paris, 1995

nouvel

The office of Architectures Jean Nouvel (AJN) closes off a street in the 11th arrondissement of Paris, a common urban configuration in that district of the French capital. Dating back to the seventeenth century, the central part of the property was originally built as the residence of the Duke of Angoulême. In the nineteenth century, symmetrical wings were added to accommodate small manufacturing businesses. On the main façade there is still a plaque reading *Maroquinerie* (Leather Shop).

In 1995 Nouvel purchased the premises and decided to move in. The architect respected the old shell of the building, but endowed it with a new interior layout, including a galvanized steel stair. The studio is organized on four levels above the ground-floor reception. These are equipped with parallel services so that they can operate independently. Each floor contains an open area with rows of drafting stations in the main space, flanked by enclosed offices, conference rooms, archives, support services, and administration housed in the generously fenestrated, intimately scaled wings. All the walls are white; the partitions enclosing the conference rooms are clad with paving stones.

Skylights wash the top-floor studio with light, which filters down to lower floors via the stairwell. The ambient light afforded in this manner alleviates the imbalance between the extensive windows on the front façade and the opaque rear wall.

On the ground floor the reception area is relatively spare. Some of the furniture occupying it was designed by Nouvel himself, including a cabinet and the "Less" table for Cartier.

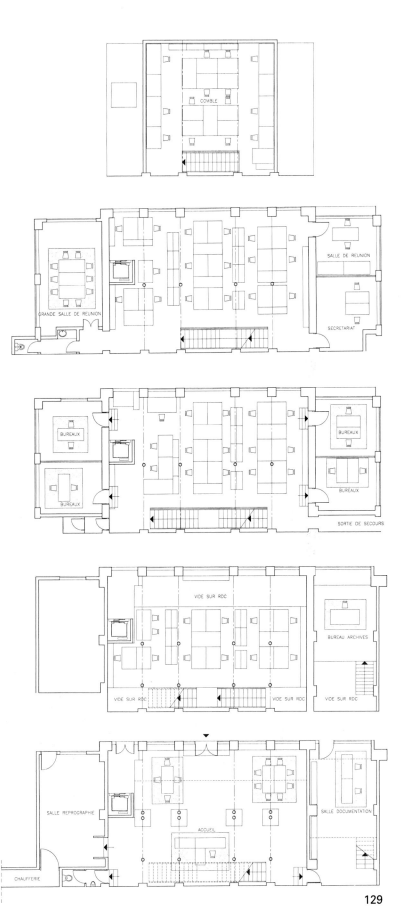

129

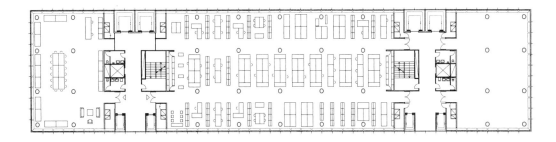

Perrault's industrial hotel, straddling the intersection of major infrastructure systems, inaugurates a new building type for Paris.

Dominique Perrault
Paris, 1990

In 1990 the Société Anonyme de Gestion Immobilière held a competition for the design of a new type of building, an "industrial hotel" capable of accommodating diverse activities on a site besieged by high-traffic roads and railways, located between the Quai d'Ivry gate to Paris and the Gare d'Austerlitz.

The winning architect, Dominique Perrault, proposed a glass curtain-wall building capable of sheltering forty companies and 500 persons. The ten-story, 17,000-square-meter (183,000-square-foot) structure is double glazed, effecting a 35-decibel reduction of noise from the surrounding environment. The window-wall panels are supported on rails directly connected to the floorplates, so that wind loads are transferred to the main structure.

Perrault's office, an open space resembling a large industrial bay, occupies the seventh floor of the building. The periphery is lined with metal shelves, mounted on tracks aligned with the window mullions, intended for storage of models and plans. Shades are affixed to the shelving, affording those workstations close to the periphery some protection from direct sunlight. Most of the designers, however, work at long drafting tables arrayed in the main space between dual service cores.

None of the windows are operable; the floors are ventilated via circular ducts that are the only visible component of the mechanical systems. The rest are hidden by stretched canvas panels forming the ceiling.

Surrounded by a snarl of expressways and rail lines, Perrault's building stands crisp and transparent; it sets up a visual exchange that works both ways, revealing its inner workings while affording an overview of the bustle outside. As a building that acknowledges its surroundings, Perrault's industrial hotel heralds a new approach toward our cities' sprawling infrastructures as potential sites for architecture.

One end of the floor is reserved for meetings, presentations, and model displays.

On a terraced slope, the architect built his third studio as a figural and literal greenhouse.

Renzo Piano
Vesima, Genoa, 1994

piano

The coastal highway leading from Genoa to the Italian Riviera is a narrow strip hemmed between steep green hills and the Mediterranean Sea. Renzo Piano chose a spectacular property along this road, some thirteen miles north of the city, as the site for the construction of his third office. (The architect maintains two others in the old quarter of Genoa and in Paris.)

Located on the terraced shoulders of the hill, the studio is configured as a tiered greenhouse that steps down the slope. Designers working at drafting stations and meeting tables dispersed among the terraced levels are connected by sightlines, and by extended indoor and outdoor stairs running parallel along one side of the building. Thanks to the structure's glazed envelope, they enjoy dazzling vistas of the sea from virtually every vantage point. Mechanically operated adjustable shades, mounted on the exterior of the sloping roof panes, ensure protection from glare and heat.

Adjoining the new structure is an existing farmhouse, sporting the colored stucco and terra-cotta indigenous to the region, which has been converted to a guest house.

It is a measure of the architect that no aspect of the architectural experience of this project has been overlooked, and nowhere is Piano's choreographic bent more evident than in the approach to the studio: visitors park at the side of the highway, and from there they are raised in a glass elevator, traveling on a funicular track up the side of the hill. One alights, heart pounding, at a small landing adjacent to the reception area on the greenhouse's middle level.

Piano's design for the studio (conceived initially as a workshop for the investigation of new materials and building methods) is characteristic of his *oeuvre* in the way it synthesizes a complex response to the site, a penchant for technology, and a strong concept of space, to arrive at a workplace that is both inspirational and humane.

The roof is protected by adjustable shades. From certain angles, the sea is a backdrop to the floor.

Main conference room on the lowest tier.

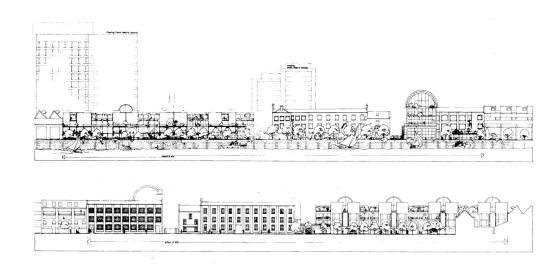

Richard Rogers
London, 1984–1989

The studio occupies part of an old refinery by the Thames.

Thames Wharf is an old refinery located on the north bank of the Thames River in the Fulham district of London, formerly an industrial area and today a residential neighborhood. The brick complex comprised a series of bays, to which the Dickhams Oil Company added warehouses to meet the needs of its growing production.

The office of Richard Rogers and Lifschutz Davidson adapted the refinery to a mixed use (residential and office), with over 16,000 square feet occupied by architecture and design studios in the more representative portions of the original buildings. The design complex consists of two large Victorian warehouses fronting the street. The main entrance is on the river façade, and is reached through a landscaped zone overlooking the water.

The property that today accommodates the Rogers office consists of a new nine-story building on the river and part of the original turn-of-the-century structure. In a wing of the old three-story industrial building are the studio reception area, computer rooms, and conference and presentation rooms.

In 1989 the architects added a barrel-vaulted glass enclosure to the roof of a 1950 building, gaining another studio floor with an inserted platform mezzanine. The new structure, supported by a series of prefabricated metal arches, was intended to open views to the north, while using diverse mechanisms to avoid the hothouse effect. Blinds on both sides are activated by panels that capture solar energy. On the west façade the vault is covered by a series of blinds gathered on a mast deployed by an electric motor.

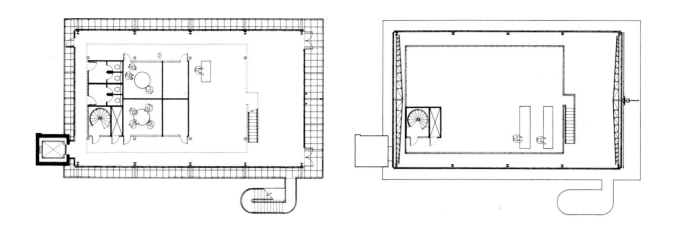

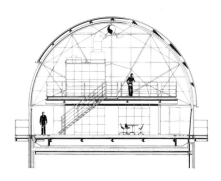

The semicircular vault was added in 1989. A set of blinds, mounted on a mast and activated by an electric motor, collects solar energy.

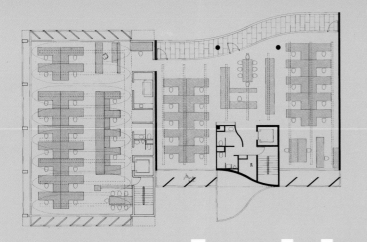

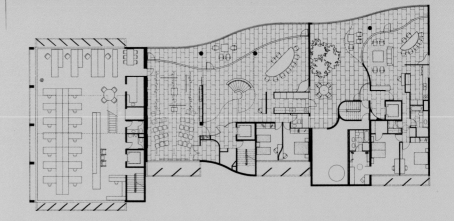

Harry Seidler
Sydney, 1973–1989

seidler

Harry Seidler's offices occupy two floors of the
building and an additional reception area on the
ground floor.

The office building at Milsons Point, on
the north shore of the port of Sydney, was
designed by Harry Seidler & Associates
and completed in time to celebrate the
25th anniversary of the firm in 1973. The
reinforced concrete structure had eight
stories, including five floors of offices, two
parking levels, and a ground-floor reception. In 1989 Seidler added a two-story
apartment penthouse, accessible via a
separate stair.

Seidler's offices occupy two floors in
addition to the street-level reception.
These are spacious, column-free work
areas, adaptable to various layouts, and
designed to capitalize on the natural light
and views available on that site. To mark
off individual work areas, the architect
used a series of storage units and furnishings that enclose the designers without
blocking the view of the open office floor.
The main offices and conference rooms on
the mezzanine occupy spaces similar to
those of the drafting and design areas;
only the diversity of the furniture—polished black granite tables and black
leather upholstered chairs—marks a subtle

hierarchy. Also on the mezzanine is Seidler's office, which is connected by a concrete platform to a landscaped terrace.

The bright Australian sunlight enters
the interior somewhat softened, having
bounced off canted *brise-soleil* louvers on
the exterior of the building. To heighten the
luminous quality of the space, the interior
walls and finishes are white, the floors are
dark gray, and the furniture is light gray.

In many early projects, Seidler was
known to draw some of his inspiration from
paintings. His influences are clearly shown
on the studio walls: works by Josef Albers,
Frank Stella, Roy Lichtenstein, and Kenneth
Noland add the only touches of color to the
building's muted palette; the juxtaposition
echoes Seidler's comprehension of architecture as an art form tempered with stringent
discipline, which he forged in his tutelage
with Gropius and Breuer.

The clarity of the architect's forms, and
his seamless integration of climatic, structural, material, and site-related considerations into the design, bear out what Seidler
called "the happy marriage between social
use, aesthetics, and technology."

The building was constructed in concrete. Several of the components are prefabricated.

Access stairway to the new addition to the building.

Detail of terra-cotta ornamentation of Sullivan's only building in New York.

SITE
New York, 1984

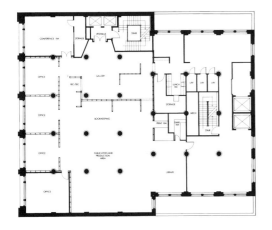

The Bayard Building of 1898 is the only structure Louis Sullivan ever realized in New York. The intricately ornamental terra-cotta façade is protected as a historic landmark, yet the floor housing the studio of SITE is the only space that preserves details of Sullivan's original interior.

At the time the group of architects designed their workplace, they gave priority to creating an open space in which they could develop their collective creative work and display the greatest possible number of designs. Because the floor intended for the offices had been occupied until 1983 by a small factory, restoring Sullivan's capitals, columns, and moldings became a concern.

Once an open space was achieved and the original ornamentation was restored, the entire studio (including the wood floors) was painted white and varnished; as in other works by the group, this has a somewhat surreal effect, suggesting the presence of a phantasmal past. The mesh partitions were manipulated to effect varying degrees of transparency. The walls' spectrum of densities and the shifting lighting conditions add narrative qualities to the monochrome space. The team's device for exhibiting plans and drawings evolved into a design prototype for a museum display system.

The architects retained the original plaster moldings
and redivided the space with semitransparent panels.

Studio entrance and project exhibition space.

Alvaro Siza
Oporto, 1996

Siza

Alvaro Siza's project sprang from the needs of a group of Oporto architects. Situated amid noisy urban chaos, the studios of Fernando Távora, Rogério Cavaca, Eduardo Souto, and Siza himself were antiquated and confined. Traffic congestion was making access to the studios more and more difficult for both clients and employees. For their new workshops, the designers purchased a lot facing the Douro River, and razed the abandoned building that occupied it. On the Rua do Aleixo a team-designed building was erected: Alvaro Siza, the primary author of the design, counted on the advice and suggestions of his partners in the venture, three of today's most distinguished Portuguese architects.

The building, an angular, five-story concrete box, accommodates several commercial premises on the ground floor; offices and studios of unaffiliated architects and engineers are housed on the first floor. The U-shaped project faces south, and has an area of nearly 3000 square meters (32,000 square feet). Wrapping the building around a relatively small court-yard increased the exposures on the upper floors. The walls and ceilings are stuccoed and the floor is covered with linoleum. Beyond those interior finishes, each designer determined the decoration and furnishings of his studio according to his own needs.

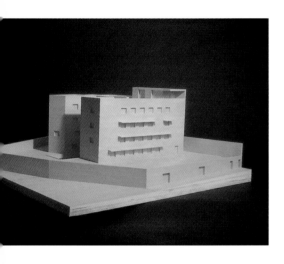

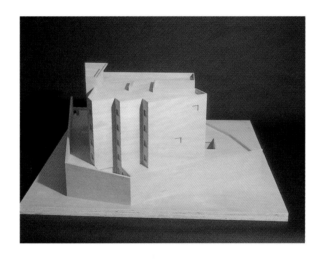

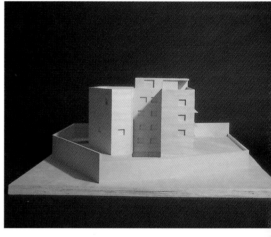

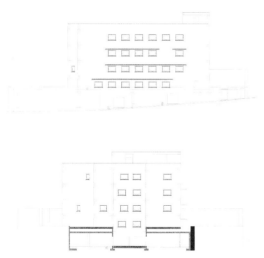

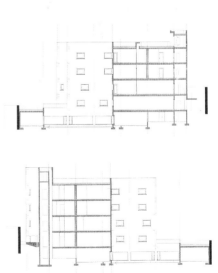

Robert A. M. Stern
New York, 1985

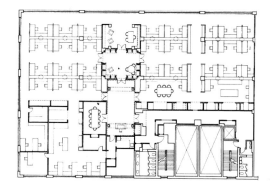

Surrounded by old factories, in sight of the Hudson River, the old warehouse loft housing Robert A. M. Stern's Manhattan studio is outfitted as a candid exercise in the application of style.

Stern contrived a main hub that alludes to the ceremonial space of a dwelling and, at the same time, represents the nature of the design regularly developed by the firm. The figural entrance, reception, and display area, considered the most formal space in the office, was designed in the classical Ionic order. The adjacent volume along the (somewhat off-center) axis holds the library. Its design, too, reflects the neo-classical approach often taken by the firm in its treatment of interiors. The offices of the managing partners open out on two expansive drafting rooms, which enjoy city and river panoramas.

To emphasize the contrast between the original building and the architectural intervention, Stern left the warehouse ceiling and the peripheral bearing walls unpainted. The two open studios are illuminated by pairs of enormous "Doric" lamps stationed on the partitions separating the drafting tables. Stern's own studio is housed in an open space that contains an enclosed conference room where the architects make their design presentations.

Clockwise, from top left: the library, reception, and studio.

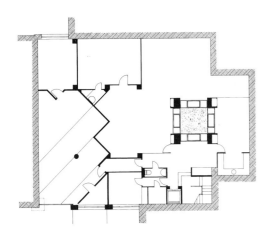 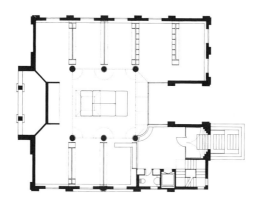 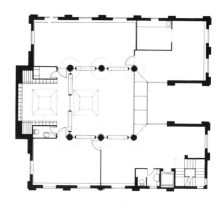

Oscar Tusquets
Barcelona, 1992

tusquets

Before moving to Villa Andrea, the property housing the residence of Oscar Tusquets, his architect's office, designer's workshop, and painter's studio, the firm of Tusquets, Díaz & Asociados had four studios scattered around Barcelona. The possibility of creating a building capable of accommodating all three callings prompted the Catalan architect to construct his own office.

Laid out on three floors, the architecture office is centered around a double-height space on the first and second floors that strikes a compromise between the privacy of each of the architects and the communication desirable in a community of designers.

On the basement floor, in addition to a garage and other services, Tusquets, Díaz & Asociados organized the firm's structural design department around a small stand of bamboos.

An elevator with a transparent ceiling, and a corner staircase beside the main entrance take care of vertical circulation; a translucent bridge covers the distance between the ground-floor administration area, the model gallery, and Tusquets's work space. These functions, together with the office of Carlos Díaz and the architects' library, surround the atrium, enabling all to enjoy outside views.

Appropriately for one who blurs the boundaries between creative disciplines, the architect furnished his studio with chairs, shelves, bookcases, and lighting of his own design.

A double-height central atrium serves a twofold function as a presentation room and a work area.

The basement accommodates the computers.

The library.

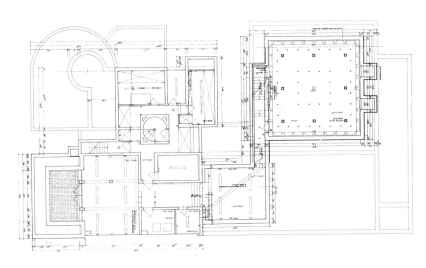

Oswald Mathias Ungers
Cologne, 1958–1989

To house an addition to his architecture studio, Oswald Mathias Ungers appended a new wing to the residence he had built for himself in 1958. The original construction, an example of the brutalism that characterized the architectural production of the time, was defined by its severity of form and absence of ornamentation. The concrete and brick exteriors were softened in the interiors with wood veneer and pure white walls. The layout of the building divided the space into rooms of different sizes with varied openings and diverse lighting conditions. The architect's first studio occupied part of this original, irregular building constructed around a center courtyard. The most recent addition complements the credo that the architect had expressed in the 1950s and summarizes four decades of practice.

The addition is a perfect cube, whose interior walls are lined with the architect's rare book collection. Ungers wanted to construct a fundamental architectural element to shelter the whimsical architectural volumes that he had hoarded for more than forty years. Contained within the platonic polyhedron, a skeletal post-and-beam structure, painted white, represents the essence of construction. A courtyard with columns in the manner of a peristyle forms the connection between the two buildings.

In front of the studio compound, occupying an equivalent area, is a garden of fruit trees, flowers, and aromatic plants, punctuated by a dark pool. Evergreen trees form a green buffer between Ungers's enclave and the neighboring structures.

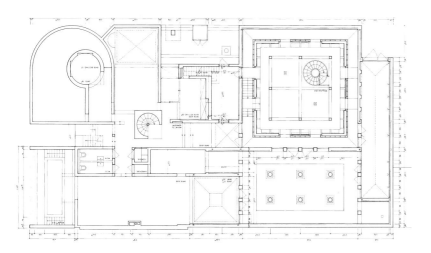

The approach to the library, and a view of the library interior.

venturi

Venturi, Scott-Brown and Associates
Manayunk, Pennsylvania, 1980

The office of Venturi, Scott-Brown and Associates (VSBA), located in the Manayunk industrial zone near Philadelphia, is vast: the architecture studio fully occupies a remodeled industrial building with four floors of 1800 square meters (19,400 square feet) each.

The ceilings are high; VSBA gutted the shell and left the space open like a loft. Wide windows and layout flexibility enable the firm to adapt the space to the different commissions occupying its employees. The arrangement of the studio changes with the size of the jobs and their requirements.

In the basement of the old building, Robert Venturi and Denise Scott-Brown incorporated a workshop for the construction of architectural models. It functions also as a laboratory/carpentry shop in which building materials are tested. In addition, the office has a photography studio and lab, with a photographer always on hand. The designers take special pride in their archive, which contains a trove of more than 80,000 photographs and drawings.

The model production area. The interior layout is adaptable to the size of commissions.

The studio occupies four floors of an old industrial building.

Before (far right), and after: early in the century, the building was a furniture showroom.

Jean-Michel Wilmotte
Paris, 1991

Near the Bastille, in a traditional neighborhood of cabinetmakers, the building housing Jean-Michel Wilmotte's architecture studio was, at the turn of the century, a furniture merchant's showroom. To align the façade of the building with the adjoining structures, Wilmotte substituted part of the original structure with a light construction of stainless steel and glass panels. On the top floors of the property he maintained the original structure and only widened the window openings.

In the interior Wilmotte set aside the ground floor as a sales showroom, visible from the street, displaying the innovative furniture designed by the firm. The building foyer was used for two reception areas, one serving the entire building and another used by the architecture studio. All the furnishings for the studio were designed by the architects working there.

Located in the first basement are a portion of the material samples gallery, a bar, and a conference and projection room. An upper floor accommodates a research laboratory.

Vertical circulation takes place in a stair encased by translucent glass panels that insulate the passage between floors without interrupting the stream of light that floods the building.

Wilmotte considers his studio a manifesto of his design preferences: these can be seen in the structure's simplicity of lines and forms; the interrelationship of spaces; the choice of primitive or partially crafted materials; and the generous proportions of the openings that connect the building to the outside. The studio invites light into the very core of the building, illustrating Wilmotte's conviction that a structure should never break the continuum between interior and exterior spaces.

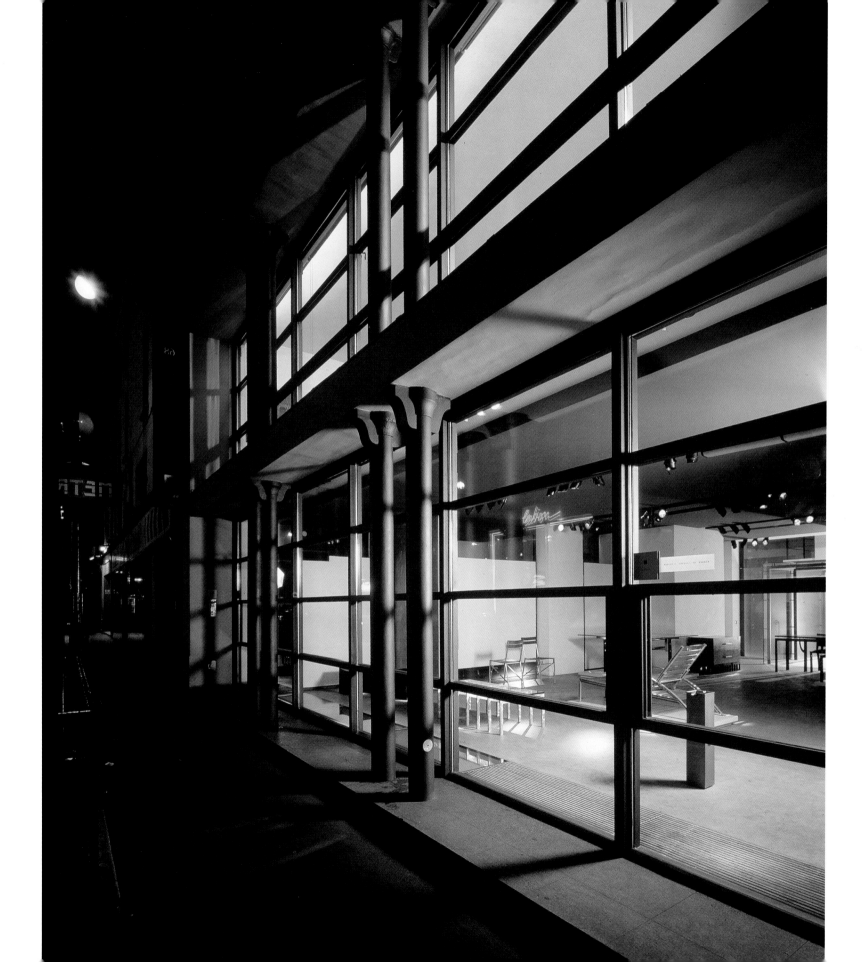

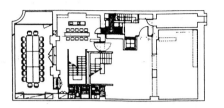
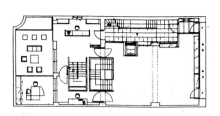
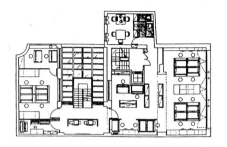

Original framing was replaced by steel.

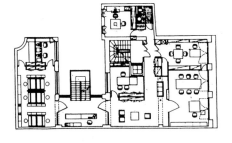
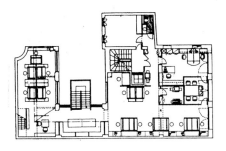

Shoei Yoh
Tokyo, 1971

For years, Shoei Yoh's studio was housed in a bermed structure of reinforced concrete that the architect had built at the foot of a small hill. Some time after its construction, Yoh erected his residence on an adjoining piece of land farther up the slope, and connected the two buildings by means of a garden. The two constructions are in stark contrast to one another: the studio was essentially a confined space, shut off from the world in order to facilitate the designer's concentration; the residence is of glass and steel—a transparent shelter set amid vistas of the surrounding landscape.

Going up and down staircases, traversing the garden that links both structures, Yoh allowed twenty-five years to pass. With time, as his children grew and his projects expanded, the architect's work invaded the transparent house. The children became independent, the designer moved with his wife to a new glass house with views of the sea, and the old enclosed concrete studio became Yoh's showroom and archive.

Most of the elements furnishing both spaces were designed by the architect himself. They are simple pieces devised, in Yoh's own words, "not to attract attention," because only simple things stand the test of time, and because when living in a glass house surrounded by vegetation, no decoration is capable of surpassing the views outside.

Stairway connecting the
architect's studio with his
residence.

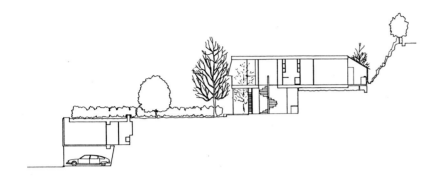

Almost all the furniture and furnishings were designed by Yoh himself. An exception:
the Wassily chairs by Marcel Breuer.

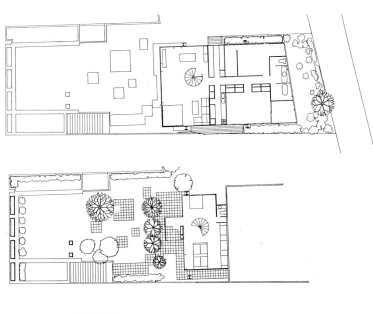

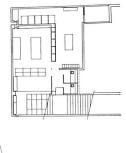

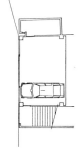

Biographies

Tadao Ando

Born in Osaka, Japan, in 1941, Tadao Ando is a self-taught architect who learned the craft over seven years spent traveling in Europe, North America, and Africa. Following his return, he established his own studio in Osaka in 1967. Ando's work, in which he borrows from both traditional Japanese culture and Modernism, has earned him numerous awards, among them the coveted Pritzker Prize in 1995. Tadao Ando has been a visiting professor at Yale, Columbia, and Harvard Universities.

Baufrösche

The "Flying Frogs" group was established in Kassel, Germany, in 1978 by Marcel Monard and Michael Wilkens. The team has seven partners of varied ages, all of them German architects: Michael Wilkens, Manfred Lenhart, Gottfried Faulstich, Elke Bolland, Uwe Hoegen, Berthold Rach, and Vizenz Freiherr von Feilitzsch. As creators of outstanding urban development projects for the city of Kassel, the collective seeks to humanize the characteristic lines of Modernism by using designs inspired by traditional construction. In addition to their work in the studio, some of the members of Baufrösche teach at German universities.

Ricardo Bofill

Born in Barcelona in 1939, Ricardo Bofill studied architecture in Geneva and returned to Spain in 1963 to found the Taller de Arquitectura (Architecture Workshop). After an initial series of projects, like The City in Space and Walden 7, both of which attracted international attention, the Taller de Arquitectura began a period of expansion and development of new ideas with large-scale projects abroad, mainly in France. This international exposure culminated with the opening of new offices in Paris, Montpellier, and New York. Among the architect's latest projects are the skyscraper at 77 W. Wacker Drive in Chicago and the Teatro Nacional de Cataluña in Barcelona.

Gerald Zugmann

David Nivière

Mario Botta

Born in Mendrisio, Ticino, in 1943, Mario Botta graduated from the Venice School of Architecture after having studied fine arts in Milan. During his training he collaborated with Le Corbusier and Louis Kahn. In 1969, he opened his own studio in Lugano, and, in 1976, began teaching as a guest professor at leading universities (École Polytechnique Fédérale of Lausanne and Yale University in New Haven). Botta's projects vary widely, from one-family houses in Ticino and the Museum of Modern Art in San Francisco (1989–1995) to Évry Cathedral in France (1988–1995).

Coop Himmelblau

Founded in Vienna in 1968 by Wolf D. Prix and Helmut Swiczinsky, Coop Himmelblau's focus extends beyond architecture to include art and design. The firm's work has been shown at the Georges Pompidou Center in Paris and at the Museum of Modern Art in New York in its "Deconstructivist Architecture" exhibition. From renovations in Vienna to urban development projects in France, the team finds teaching compatible with design. At present they are working on a fine arts academy in Munich and a health museum and a cinematography center in Dresden. Coop Himmelblau has offices in Vienna and Los Angeles.

Alexandre Chemetoff

Born in 1950 in Paris, Alexandre Chemetoff studied landscaping at the École Nationale Supérieure d'Horticulture of Versailles and graduated in 1977. In 1983 he founded the firm Bureau des Paysages. A fundamental part of his professional career revolves around landscaping and the development of public spaces. Among his latest projects are the gardens for the Palais des Congrès of Nantes (designed by Yves Lion), the Place du Marché in Vitry, and the renovation of the exterior spaces of the Darnbaise district in Venissieux. Since 1987 Alexandre Chemetoff has been a guest professor at various universities around the world and has served on numerous international juries.

David Chipperfield

After graduating from the Architectural Association of London, David Chipperfield worked at the offices of Richard Rogers and Norman Foster before establishing his own practice in 1984. In its first few years, Chipperfield's firm was internationally recognized for a number of small-scale projects and commercial interior design commissions. In 1987, Chipperfield opened an office in Tokyo where, among other projects, he has designed shops for Japanese designer Issey Miyake. Although David Chipperfield devotes most of his time to design, he has taught at such universities as Harvard, the Royal College of Art of London, and the Polytechnique Fédérale of Lausanne.

Simon Head

VISUM/Rudi Meisel

Terry Farrell

Born in Manchester in 1938, Terry Farrell trained at the University of Newcastle and then at the University of Pennsylvania, where he studied under professors Louis Kahn, Robert Venturi, and Romaldo Giurgola. Opening his own office in London in 1965, he formed a partnership with Nicholas Grimshaw, with whom he continued working until 1980. Undertaking projects that range from urban development to renovation, Farrell designed the Consulate General of the United Kingdom in Hong Kong, as well as Kowloon Station and the Peak Tower urban development project there, where he has maintained a second office since 1991. Terry Farrell has taught at universities throughout the world.

Norman Foster

Born in Manchester in 1935, Norman Foster attended the university there before completing his studies at Yale. In 1963, he founded the Team 4 group with his wife, Wendy Sue Foster, and Richard Rogers. In 1967, he established Foster Associates in London. One of the most international of contemporary designers, Foster has contributed enormously to the dissemination of high technology as an architectural response to contemporary culture and production. Among his projects are the headquarters of the Hong Kong and Shanghai Bank (1979–1986), the third London airport at Stansted (1981–1991), and the remodeling of the Sackler Galleries at the Royal Academy of Arts of London. Foster Associates also handles large-scale commissions that require direction of the entire design process, from initial sketches to furniture design. In almost thirty years of professional practice, Foster Associates has received over sixty international awards.

Frank O. Gehry

Frank O. Gehry was born in Toronto in 1929 and trained in the United States before establishing his own practice in 1962. In addition to his famous house in Santa Monica—touted as the inspiration for a new California architecture—Gehry designed other buildings with a strong sculptural component, like the Vitra Museum in Weil, Germany, the Aerospace Museum of California, the Psychiatric Institute at Yale, the Children's Museum in Boston, and the new Guggenheim in Bilbao. Gehry is currently working on several cultural centers in some Eastern European countries and Middle-Eastern capitals. A designer of furniture, lamps, and interiors, Frank O. Gehry was awarded the Pritzker Prize in 1989.

Michael Graves

Born in Indianapolis in 1934, Michael Graves studied architecture at the University of Cincinnati and then at the Harvard Graduate School of Design. He was also granted a fellowship at the American Academy in Rome. A founding member of the New York Five, together with Peter Eisenman, John Hejduk, Richard Meier, and Charles Gwathmey, Graves departed from the Modernist tradition, choosing to instead revise and update traditional architectural forms. Graves' work in product and furniture design is exhibited in many international museums. Michael Graves has received fifteen Progressive Architecture Awards and, since 1962, has taught at Princeton University.

Nello Brancaccio

Vittorio Gregotti

Born in Novara, Italy, in 1927, Vittorio Gregotti founded Gregotti Associati in Milan in 1974. The firm, led by partners Augusto Cagnardi and Pierluigi Cerri, engages in architecture, urban planning, and graphic and industrial design, as well as naval architecture. The bulk of Gregotti's commissions occur in Italy, Portugal, Spain, France, Belgium, Algeria, Japan, and the United States. For years the founding partners have balanced their architectural work with their extensive publishing activities. Although Gregotti's designers work as a team on a variety of projects, the partners have gradually developed specializations: Gregotti and Cagnardi are engaged in architectural and urban development work, while Cerri is in charge of graphic and industrial design.

Nicholas Grimshaw

Nicholas Grimshaw was born in Hove, England, in 1939. In 1980 he established his practice after having been recognized internationally for his industrial buildings for Citroën, Zanussi, Herman Miller, and BMW. Today, Grimshaw's London office works on projects covering a broad typological spectrum, from sports pavilions to commercial buildings and urban development. Among his major projects are the Financial Times Printing Works, the Waterloo international terminal for the Channel Tunnel in London, and the new stock exchange building in Berlin. Grimshaw maintains that architectural form must reflect the function of the building. He has received a wide range of prizes for his ergonomic designs.

Gwathmey Siegel

Born in Charlotte, North Carolina, in 1938, Charles Gwathmey graduated from Yale University in 1962 and went on to become a member of the New York Five during the 1970s. Robert Siegel completed his studies at Harvard in 1963. The two main partners of the New York firm opened their own studio in 1968. Since then, the office has carried out more than 150 projects all over the world. Prominent in its extensive portfolio are several office buildings and the expansion and renovation of New York's Guggenheim Museum which, in the opinion of the designers, proved that "thorough research can enrich even a masterpiece." Among other awards, the enlargement of the Frank Lloyd Wright building won Gwathmey and Siegel the American Institute of Architects prize. At present, they are working on the design of a museum for the University of Washington.

Zaha Hadid

Born in Baghdad in 1950, Zaha Hadid graduated from the Architectural Association of London in 1977. She then worked as a member of the OMA (Office for Metropolitan Architecture) side by side with Rem Koolhaas and Elia Zenghelis. In 1979, she opened her own studio, from which she has embarked on a remarkable mission of conceptual and formal renewal of architecture. The difficulty of her projects and the beauty of her plans had for years earned her the sobriquet of "paper architect." Until she completed Monsoon restaurant in Sapporo, Japan, in the early nineties, her only finished project was the interior remodeling of an apartment on Eaton Place. However, in recent years she has completed several projects, among them a fire station in Vitra, Germany. A frequent lecturer, Hadid has taught at numerous international universities.

Agustín Hernández

Agustín Hernández graduated from the National School of Architecture of the University of Mexico City in 1954. A professor there since 1957, Hernández has elaborated his own architectural theory in which he combines the guidelines of Modernism with his own Mexican culture, as well as with the new materials made possible by modern industry. In addition to designing the Mexican pavilion at the Osaka International Exposition of 1970, his works have been published by numerous international journals and have won him many awards, including the Dom international prize (Cologne, Germany) and the gold medal at the Second Mexico City Biennial in 1991.

Michael Hopkins

The Michael Hopkins & Partners architecture studio was founded in London in 1976. Today it has five partners: Patricia Hopkins, John Pringle, Ian Sharratt, Bill Taylor, and Michael Hopkins. The firm's work is characterized by the use of the most current construction technologies together with a personal reinterpretation of traditional materials. Projects range from the remodeling of the Victoria and Albert Museum, the remodeling of and addition to the Schlumberger Research Laboratories in Cambridge, and the design of the Glyndebourne Opera House. Sir Michael Hopkins has been a member of the Royal Academy since 1992, and in 1994 received the Prince Philip Prize for designer of the year and the Royal Gold Medal of Architecture.

Arata Isozaki

Arata Isozaki was born in Oita, Japan, in 1931. After studying architecture in Tokyo, he worked with Kenzo Tange for nearly ten years until 1963 when he founded Isozaki & Associates. Designer of countless houses, including several examples of experimental residential architecture, Isozaki is the architect of the Modern Art Museum in Gunma, Japan, the Museum of Contemporary Art in Los Angeles, the Palau Sant Jordi in Barcelona, and the Team Disney Building in Orlando, Florida. Among the numerous international prizes that Isozaki has received are the annual prize of the Institute of Architects of Japan, the R.I.B.A. Gold Medal, and the F.A.D.T. of Architecture.

Josef Paul Kleihues

Born in Rheine, Westphalia, in 1933, Josef Paul Kleihues graduated from the Universities of Stuttgart and Berlin in 1957 and 1959 respectively. Since 1986 he has held the chair of City Planning and Design at the University of Dortmund, where he has headed the Department of Architectural Design and Theory since 1973. In 1975, he established the journal *Dortmunder Architekturhefte,* which he edited until 1983. In recent years, he has taught at Cooper Union in New York and at the Kunstakademie of Dusseldorf and has served as director of the International Bauausstellung Berlin (IBA). He received the Berliner Architekturpreis in 1994 and the Deutscher Natursteinspreis in 1995. Noteworthy projects are the Prehistory Museum of Frankfurt, the Public Galleries of Sindelfingen and Kornwetheim, and the new Contemporary Art Museum in Chicago.

Philippe Vermès

Scagliola/Brakkee

Ricardo Legorreta

Mexican-born Ricardo Legorreta founded his own studio in Mexico City in 1963. A second studio, opened in 1977 in Los Angeles, specializes in furniture and accessories, and Legorreta Arquitectos, also in Los Angeles, opened in 1985. Legorreta has overseen many restorations and designed several museums, libraries, research centers, and residences in the United States and Mexico, the Cathedral of Managua, and hotels in Mexico City, as well as a number of urban planning projects. Since 1969, he has lectured at some of the leading universities of Mexico, Spain, Japan, the United States, Colombia, Argentina, and Chile.

Yves Lion

Born in Casablanca in 1945, Yves Lion designed a housing prototype, the Maison d'Habitation, which a real estate company markets. In addition to numerous public buildings (schools, courthouses, and apartment buildings), the architect has worked on urban renovation projects. Among his latest commissions are the Palais des Congrès of Nantes (1986–1991), the Palais de Justice of Lyons (1981–1995), and Cité Descarte, a public housing development of more than 200 units (1987–1995). Lion has been a member of numerous international juries and has lectured at various European and American universities. He is a professor at the Paris-Tolbiac School of Architecture.

Thom Mayne (Morphosis)

After studying at the Harvard Graduate School of Design, Thom Mayne spent a year at the American Academy in Rome. Along with Michael Rotondi, he founded Morphosis, one of the United States' most innovative architecture firms. (Rotondi has since left to pursue his own practice.) As head of Morphosis, Mayne collaborates with colleagues Mark MacVay, John Enright, Blythe Alison, Kim Groves, Janet Sager, and Eui-Sung Yi. He has taught at Washington University in St. Louis, University of Texas at Austin, U.C.L.A., Harvard, and Yale, among others.

Mecanoo

The Dutch firm Mecanoo, made up of Henk Döll, Chris de Weijer, Francine Houben, and, formerly, Erick van Egeraat, has designed numerous public housing projects, prototype houses, and commercial buildings. The firm has also done a great deal of urban development work. Recent projects include the Herdenkingsplein housing in Maastricht, a pleasure pavilion in Rotterdam, and the restoration of a Neo-Renaissance building in Budapest for Nationale Nederlanden Hungary and ING Bank.

Giovanni Zanzi

Lewis Baltz

Nicolas Tavernier

Richard Meier

Born in Newark, New Jersey, in 1934, Richard Meier graduated from Cornell University and established his practice in New York in 1963. A 1984 winner of the Pritzker Prize, Meier is noted for his museum work—Frankfurt Museum, Contemporary Art Museum of Barcelona, High Museum of Art in Atlanta—and civic buildings—the new city hall in The Hague, the Federal Courthouse in Phoenix. Meier is now completing the Getty Center for the Arts on the outskirts of Los Angeles.

Enric Miralles

Enric Miralles was born in Barcelona in 1955. He received his doctorate from that city's Escuela Superior de Arquitectura, where he now teaches. Considered one of the leaders of contemporary Spanish architecture, his projects evoke a diverse and highly personal approach toward planning and resources. His Igualada Cemetery, Huesca Sports Palace, and the School of Morelia are particularly noteworthy. Miralles has also taught at Harvard, Columbia, the B.T.H. of Frankfurt, and Princeton University.

Benedetta Tagliabue studied architecture in Venice and began her doctoral studies in New York, where she applied her special skill in restoration to various projects. Since 1992 she has shared an architectural practice with Enric Miralles and, in addition to engaging in publishing activities, is completing her doctorate.

Jean Nouvel

Born in Fumel, France, in 1945, Jean Nouvel graduated from the École Nationale Supérieur des Beaux Arts in Paris in 1966 with degrees in architecture and town planning. Very active in the French cultural scene of the 1980s, Nouvel founded several architectural organizations, including Architectes Mouvement Mars 1976 and Syndicat de l'Architecture. For Nouvel, architecture expresses time by capturing a moment in the history of civilization. Among his major projects are the Institut du Monde Arabe in Paris, the Opéra de Lyon, and the recently inaugurated Cartier Foundation in Paris. He has received numerous international awards.

Dominique Perrault

Dominique Perrault studied at the UP6 School of Architecture in Paris, from which he obtained a degree in town planning in 1977 and another in architecture in 1978. In 1980 he earned a Master's in History. One of the youngest members of today's French architectural community, Perrault won the competition for construction of the Bibliothèque Nationale de France at barely thirty years of age. The planning of that building launched his international reputation as an architect, and his career has since been marked by new commissions in foreign cities (Velodrome and olympic swimming pool in Berlin) and by his work in urban planning (development of the Tremblay-en-France and Bordeaux urban centers). A recent project is the Great Conservatory in the City of Science and Industry of Paris.

Seiji Okumiya

David Moore

Renzo Piano

Born in Genoa in 1937, Renzo Piano graduated from Milan Polytechnic in 1964. From 1965 to 1970 he worked with Louis Kahn in Philadelphia. What followed in 1971 was a partnership with Richard Rogers, which culminated in the construction of the Georges Pompidou Center in Paris in 1977. Piano and Rogers went their separate ways in 1977, and the Italian architect then began a three-year collaboration with Peter Rice. In 1980 Piano founded the Renzo Piano Building Workshop, a studio laboratory where the designer researched organic structures and materials. Piano opened a studio in Paris in 1987 and, two years later, an office in Osaka, Japan, where he designed the Kansai Airport. Principal works include the museum for the Menil collection in Houston, the Museum of American Art in Los Angeles, the revitalization of the old port of Genoa, and the adaptive use of the Lingotto Building in Turin.

Richard Rogers

After graduating from the Architectural Association of London, Richard Rogers studied architecture at Yale. During the 1960s, he was a member of the Team Four group, to which Norman Foster also belonged. In the early 1970s, Rogers became associated with John Young, Marco Goldsmid, and Mike Davis, and followed an architectural path that led the group to deal with the most diverse architectural and urban planning problems: from industrial buildings to airports, corporate headquarters and cultural centers, laboratories and site-sensitive urban development. Among the numerous works in Rogers' portfolio are the Georges Pompidou Center in Paris (with Renzo Piano), the Lloyds Building in London, and many urban development projects in Japan and Southeast Asia. In Spain, Rogers won the competition for the Parc Bit, now being planned in Palma de Mallorca.

Harry Seidler

A native of Vienna, Harry Seidler was educated in England and received a degree in architecture from the University of Manitoba (Canada) in 1944. He then continued his studies at Harvard, where he was a student of Walter Gropius, and at Black Mountain College, where he studied with Josef Albers. After working with Marcel Breuer and Oscar Niemeyer, he opened his own studio in Australia in 1949. Designer of numerous apartment and office buildings in Australia, Seidler has also worked in Europe, Central America, and Asia. In nearly fifty years of professional practice, he has been awarded over forty prizes. Seidler has been a guest professor at Harvard and the E.T.H. of Zurich, and has lectured at many universities.

SITE

Founded in New York in 1970 by James Wines, Alison Sky, and Michelle Stone, SITE (short for "sculpture in the environment") focused on the dematerialization of architecture complemented by a dose of good humor. Their many designs for Best Products, in which the buildings appeared unfinished or in various stages of disrepair, are characteristic of their approach. While they worked on innovative architecture and design projects, the three principal members also published architecture books and collaborated with contemporary art magazines. Most of SITE's work is confined to commercial buildings and public spaces. The group disbanded in 1993, and its members continue to practice independently.

Alvaro Siza
Born in Matozinhos, Portugal, in 1933, Alvaro Siza studied at the Oporto School of Fine Arts and worked with Fernando Távora until 1958. In 1954 he also opened his own studio in Oporto. Siza's keen interest in public housing led to commissions for apartment buildings in Kreuzberg-Berlin and Amsterdam. A recipient of the Pritzker Prize in 1992, his latest projects include the Meteorology Center of Barcelona's Olympic City and the Galician Center of Contemporary Art in Santiago de Compostela. Siza has taught architecture at his alma mater in Oporto since 1965.

Robert A.M. Stern
Born in New York in 1939, Robert A.M. Stern studied at Columbia and received his degree in architecture from Yale in 1965. As Principal of Robert A.M. Stern Architects, he presides over a firm with over sixty employees. Designers of countless residences, corporate headquarters, institutional buildings, and several of the unique and charismatic projects for the Walt Disney Company, the firm's work is concentrated mainly in the United States and Asia. Stern is a professor at Columbia University and the author of numerous books.

Oscar Tusquets Guillen
Architect by training, painter by inclination, and designer by vocation, Oscar Tusquets Guillen thinks of himself as a "complete" artist. After studying drafting, he graduated from the Escuela Superior de Arquitectura of Barcelona in 1965, and later founded the Per Studio and the Empresa Productora B.D. Ediciones de Diseño. Until 1984 he collaborated with architect Lluís Clotet and in 1987 formed Tusquets, Díaz & Asociados, a firm in which Carlos Díaz organizes and manages the projects. Though his architectural work has been primarily confined to Spain, Tusquets' excellent design ability is respected worldwide.

Oswald Mathias Ungers
Born in Kaiseresch, Germany, in 1926, Oswald Mathias Ungers practiced in his own architecture studio in Cologne before teaching architecture at Cornell, Harvard, the Universities of Berlin, Vienna, Dusseldorf, and San Lucca (Rome), and U.C.L.A. In 1971 he was named a member of the American Institute of Architects. Included in numerous biennials and "Documenta" exhibitions, the work of Ungers is highly representative of contemporary German institutional architecture. His major projects include museums and institutions in Cologne, Berlin, Bremen, and Frankfurt.

Boulat/Sipa Presse

Robert Venturi
Born in Philadelphia in 1925, Robert Venturi collaborated with Louis Kahn and Eero Saarinen before founding his own studio in 1964. His publication of *Complexity and Contradiction in Architecture* in 1966 established him as one of architecture's foremost Postmodern theorists. In 1967, **Denise Scott-Brown** joined Venturi to form Venturi, Scott-Brown & Associates, a firm with over fifty employees. Venturi, the company's design director, was awarded the Pritzker Prize in 1991, years after the studio as a whole received an award from the A.I.A. for the influence it exercised over modern architecture. Projects include Gordon Wu Hall at Princeton University, the Sainsbury Wing of the National Gallery in London, and the Seattle Art Museum.

Jean-Michel Wilmotte
After establishing a practice in Paris in 1975, Jean-Michel Wilmotte opened a second office in Tokyo. Both headquarters are staffed by a total of fifty engineering, urban planning, and design professionals. Specializing in museology (the Chiado Museum in Lisbon) and in the rearrangement of public furniture (Lyons Center, Champs-Elysées, Rouen Stations, Nimes Airport), the firm designs each and every one of the components included in its projects— from public furniture and lighting fixtures to signage and buildings.

Shoei Yoh
Born in 1940 in the Japanese city of Kumamoto, Shoei Yoh studied economics in Tokyo and fine arts and applied arts at the Universities of Tokyo and Wittenberg, Ohio. In 1970 he established his own practice in Fukuoka, and in 1992 was invited to lecture as a guest professor at Columbia. Winner of various prizes, his major works include a large number of residential designs, commercial buildings, and golf courses. Yoh is currently a professor of city planning at the University of Keio.

Photography Credits

Peter Aaron/Esto, pp. 150–153, 156–157
Tadao Ando, pp. 18–21
Arcaid, pp. 48–53, 143, 56–61
Jaime Ardiles-Arce, pp. 78–79
Carla de Benedetti, pp. 70–73
Tom Bonner, pp. 123–125
Marek Bulaj, pp. 68–69
Robert Cesar/Archipress, pp. 172–175
Richard Davies, pp. 56–61, 80–83, 88–93
Arnauld Duboys Fresney, pp. 42–47
Scott Frances/Esto, pp. 113–115
Fregoso & Basalto, pp. 134–139
Ferran Freixa, pp. 116–121
Dennis Gilbert, pp. 54–55
Lisa Hammel/Fotodesign, pp. 23, 25–27
Ishida, pp. 134–139
Athos Leece, pp. 54–55
Lourdes Legorreta, pp. 102–105
Julie Marquart, pp. 168–171
Ryuji Miyamoto, pp. 94–97
Florian Monheim/Fotodesign, pp. 23, 25–27
J.M. Monthiers, pp. 106–109
Stefan M ller, pp. 164–167
Pino Musi, p. 39
Lisa Oggi, pp. 54–55
John Peck, pp. 74–77
Matteo Piazza, pp. 140–142
Markus Pillhofer, p. 41
Publifoto, pp. 134–139
Jo Reid, pp. 74–77
Christian Richters, pp. 110–111
Deidi van Schaewen, pp. 126–129, 130–133
Teresa Siza, p. 155
Yashushi Sugimata, pp. 176–181
Rafael Vargas, pp. 28–33, 159–163
HÈctor Velasco, pp. 84–87
Joshua W. White, pp. 62–67
Nigel Young, pp. 54–55
Alo Zanetta, pp. 34–39
Giovanni Zanzi, pp. 116, 119